Everyman's Poetry

Everyman, I will go with thee,
and be thy guide

Oliver Goldsmith

Selected and edited by ROBERT L. MACK

Vanderbilt University

EVERYMAN
J. M. Dent · London

This edition first published by Everyman Paperbacks in 1997
Introduction and other critical apparatus
© J. M. Dent 1997

J. M. Dent
Orion Publishing Group
Orion House
5 Upper St Martin's Lane,
London WC2H 9EA

Typeset by Deltatype Ltd, Birkenhead, Merseyside
Printed in Great Britain by
The Guernsey Press Co. Ltd, Guernsey, C. I.

British Library Cataloguing-in-Publication
Data is available upon request.

ISBN 0 460 87827 1

Contents

Note on the Author and Editor

OLIVER GOLDSMITH (1730?–74) was born in County Westmeath, Ireland and educated first at Trinity College, Dublin and subsequently at Edinburgh University, where he studied medicine. At the age of twenty-three Goldsmith embarked on a lengthy tour of the Continent, often pursuing his travels on foot and passing, in time, through Germany, Switzerland, France and northern Italy. At the age of twenty-five he settled in London, pursuing a variety of odd jobs – including work as a physician, an usher at a boys' school and a proof-reader – before beginning his career as a literary 'hack'. He had soon contributed essays and reviews to a number of publications including the *Critical Review*, *The Busy Body* and the *British Magazine*. In 1761, he met and became friends with Samuel Johnson, and was a few years later, along with Johnson, Joshua Reynolds, Edmund Burke and David Garrick, one of the founding members of The Club, an informal group of 'wits' and critics. His popular poem *The Traveller, or A Prospect of Society* was first printed in December 1764. A volume of collected *Essays* appeared the following year and 1766 saw the publication of his perennially popular sentimental novel, *The Vicar of Wakefield*. His most famous poem, *The Deserted Village*, was published in 1770 and his comedy *She Stoops to Conquer* was produced at Covent Garden in 1773. Goldsmith died while still hard at work on several projects in April 1774. In an era famed for the generic versatility of its authors, Goldsmith outshone even the most prolific writers, producing a novel, a dramatic comedy, and several poems the popular currency of which are to this very day to be envied.

ROBERT L. MACK is an Assistant Professor of English at Vanderbilt University. His publications include editions of the *Arabian Nights' Entertainments* and Horace Walpole's *The Castle of Otranto* and *Hieroglyphic Tales*. He has also edited the poetry of Thomas Gray for the Everyman's Poetry series. He is currently writing a biography of Thomas Gray.

Chronology of Goldsmith's Life

Year	Age	Life
1730?		(10 November) Born either at Pallas, County Westmeath, Ireland or at Ardnagowan – his grandmother's house – near Elphin, to the Revd Charles Goldsmith and his wife Ann (née James). The family soon moves to Lissoy (or Lishoy), where Goldsmith's childhood is spent. He is educated first at the Diocesan School at Elphin and at schools at Athlone and Edgeworthstown, County Longford

Chronology of his Times

Year	Literary Context	Historical Events
1730	Cibber made Poet Laureate Thomson completes *The Seasons* Duck, *Poems on Several Occasions*	Walpole/Townshend split
1731	Birth of Cowper Death of Defoe Pope *An Epistle to . . . Burlington* Lillo, *The London Merchant* First issue of *The Gentleman's Magazine*	
1732	Death of Gay Bentley's edition of John Milton's *Paradise Lost*	Colony of Georgia founded; Academie of Ancient Music founded
1733	Pope, *Imitations of Horace* (to 1738)	Excise Crisis; Walpole abandons scheme to reorganize the customs and impose a heavy Excise Tax
1734	Pope, *An Essay on Man*	General Election; University of Gottingen founded by George II
1735	Pope, *An Epistle to Arbuthnot* Brooke, *The Fool of Quality*	
1736		Porteous Riots in Edinburgh
1737	James and Charles Wesley, *Psalms and Hymns*	Death of Queen Caroline
1738	Johnson, *London*	

Year	Age	Life

1745   14   (11 June) Admitted as sizar to Trinity College,
              Dublin

1747   16   Death of Father. (21 May) Takes part in a student
              riot for which he earns a 'public
              admonishment'

Year	Literary Context	Historical Events
1739	Fielding, *The Champion* (to 1741) Swift, *Verses on the Death of Doctor Swift*	War (the 'War of Jenkins' Ear') declared against Spain
1740	Cibber, *An Apology for the Life of Colley Cibber* Hume, *A Treatise of Human Nature* Richardson, *Pamela* (to 1741)	War of the Austrian Succession
1741		General Election
1742	Pope, *The New Dunciad* William Collins, *Persian Eclogues* Fielding, *Joseph Andrews* Young, *The Complaint, or, Night Thoughts* (to 1745)	Walpole resigns and is created Earl of Orford
1743	Fielding, *Jonathan Wild* Blair, *The Grave*	Battle of Dettingen
1744	Death of Pope Akenside, *The Pleasure of Imagination* Warton, *The Enthusiast* Johnson, *Life of Mr Richard Savage*	Ministry of Henry Pelham
1745	Death of Swift	Jacobite Rebellion; The forces of Charles Edward, the Young Pretender ('Bonnie Prince Charlie') invade Scotland and are eventually defeated at the Battle of Culloden (1746)
1746	William Collins, *Odes on Several Descriptive and Allegoric Subjects* Warton, *Odes on Various Subjects*	
1747	Warton, *The Pleasures of Melancholy* Richardson, *Clarissa* (to 1748)	General Election

Year	Age	Life
1750	19	(February) Graduates BA
1750–52	19–21	Attempts unsuccessfully to be ordained into the Anglican Church. Considers emigrating to America (from Cork) and studying law in London. Is engaged as a private tutor to a family in County Roscommon
1752	21	(September) Admitted to Edinburgh University to study medicine
1753	22	(January) Elected to the Medical Society at Edinburgh University
1754	23	Leaves Edinburgh to pursue study of medicine at Leyden
1755	24	Travels across the Continent (for the most part on foot) stopping in Germany, Switzerland, France and northern Italy.

Year	Literary Context	Historical Events
1748	*A Collection of Poems by Several Hands* edited by Robert Dodsley Thomson, *The Castle of Indolence* Smollett, *Gil Blas*, *Roderick Random* Hume, *Philosophical Essays Concerning Human Understanding*	Peace of Aix-la-Chappelle (with France) ends the War of the Austrian Succession
1749	Fielding, *Tom Jones* Johnson, *The Vanity of Human Wishes* William Collins, *Ode on the Popular Superstitions of the Highlands of Scotland*	
1750	Johnson begins *The Rambler* (to 1752)	
1751	Birth of Richard Brinsley Sheridan Fielding, *Amelia* Smollett, *Peregrine Pickle*	Death of Frederick, Prince of Wales; succeeded as heir by his twelve-year-old son, George; Gin Act curbs excessive drinking
1752	Smart, *Poems on Several Occasions* Birth of Frances Burney Charlotte Lennox, *The Female Quixote*	Gregorian Calendar adopted
1753	Smollett, *Ferdinand, Count Fathom* Richardson, *Sir Charles Grandison* (to 1754)	French drive the English from the Ohio Valley and found Fort Duquesne (Pittsburgh); Jewish Naturalization Bill (repealed 1754)
1754	Death of Fielding	Ministry of the Duke of Newcastle
1755	Johnson, *Dictionary of the English Language* Fielding, *Journal of a Voyage to Lisbon*	

Year	Age	Life
1756	25	(1 February) Returns to England
1756–7	25–6	Engaged in various odd jobs in London and elsewhere, including positions as an apothecary, a physician, a proofreader (in the printing shop of Samuel Richardson in Salisbury Court) and an usher at a boys' school in Peckham. May have applied for and received his medical degree from Trinity College
1757	26	Writes articles for the *Monthly Review*, while lodging with its editor, Ralph Griffiths
1758	27	(February) Translates Jean Marteilhe's *Mémoires d'un Protestant* as *The Memoires of a Protestant, Condemned to the Galleys of France for his Religion*. Intends, but fails, to travel to India, where he had been promised a post as civilian physician with the East India Company
1759	28	(2 April) Publishes *An Enquiry into the Present State of Polite Learning in Europe*. Contributes essays and reviews to, among others, Tobias Smollett's *Critical Review*, *The Busy Body*, the *British Magazine*, the *Royal Magazine* and *Lady's Magazine*. (6 October–24 November) Writes the periodical *The Bee*
1760	29	(January) The 'Chinese Letters' begin publication in John Newbery's *Public Ledger*
1761	30	Meet and cultivates the acquaintance of Samuel Johnson and Joshua Reynolds

Year	Literary Context	Historical Events
1756	Birth of Godwin	Beginning of the Seven Years' War against France; Alliance of Britain and Prussia against France, Austria and Russia; William Pitt, as Minister in charge of War, prosecutes the conflict with vigour; Black Hole of Calcutta
1757	Burke, *A Philosophical Enquiry into the Origin of our Ideas of the Sublime and the Beautiful* John Dyer, *The Fleece* Birth of Blake	Victory of Clive at the Battle of Plassey (India); British hegemony in the subcontinent established
1758	Johnson, *The Idler* (to 1760)	
1759	Johnson, *Rasselas* Death of William Collins Birth of Burns	Capture of Quebec by General Wolfe; capture of Fort Duquesne by the English; British Museum opens; Wedgwood Potteries founded
1760	Sterne, *Tristram Shandy* (to 1767) James MacPherson, *Fragments of Ancient Poetry Collected in the Highlands of Scotland* Smollett, *Sir Launcelot Greaves* (to 1762) Birth of Beckford	Death of George II; accession of George III, his grandson
1761	Death of Richardson	General Election; Pitt resigns

Year	Age	Life
1762	31	The 'Chinese Letters' collected and published as *The Citizen of the World*. Publishes *The Life of Richard Nash, of Bath, Esq.* Effects his release from arrest for debt by selling (through Johnson and Newbery) a third share of *The Vicar of Wakefield* to a Salisbury bookseller, Benjamin Collins
1764	33	Founding member of The Club with, among others, Johnson, Reynolds, Edmund Burke, David Garrick and Bennet Langton. (26 June) Publishes *An History of England in a Series of Letters from a Nobleman to his Son*. Sells the manuscript of *The Captivity: an Oratorio* to Newbery and Dodsley. (19 December) Publishes *The Traveller, or A Prospect of Society*
1765	34	(3 June) Publishes collected *Essays by Mr Goldsmith*
1766	35	(27 March) *The Vicar of Wakefield* printed by Benjamin Collins, published by Francis Newbery (nephew to John Newbery)
1767	36	(April) Publishes a two-volume anthology, *The Beauties of English Poesy*. Death of John Newbery

Year	Literary Context	Historical Events
1762	Macpherson, *Fingal, an Ancient Epic Poem* Mary Collier, *Poems on Several Occasions*	Lord Bute becomes Prime Minister
1763	Smart, *A Song to David*	Peace of Paris; Canada and India ceded to Great Britain
1764	Goldsmith, *The Traveller* Walpole, *The Castle of Otranto*	James Hargreaves invents the spinning jenny
1765	Death of Edward Young Smart, *A Translation of the Psalms of David*	Lord Rockingham becomes Prime Minister; American Stamp Act passed to finance the Seven Years' War (repealed 1766); Sir William Blackstone publishes his *Commentaries on the Laws of England* (to 1769)
1766	Smollett, *Travels Through France and Italy* Percy, *Reliques of English Poetry*	Ministry of the Earl of Chatham (William Pitt); death of James Edward Stuart (the Old Pretender); Henry Cavendish discovers hydrogen
1767	Birth of Maria Edgeworth	Revenue Bill (taxing tea, glass, etc.) enacted in the American colonies

Year	Age	Life
1768	37	(29 January) *The Good Natur'd Man* performed at Covent Garden. (May) Death of his brother Henry, to whom he had dedicated *The Traveller*
1769	38	(18 May) Publishes *The Roman History*. (December) Appointed Professor of Ancient History at the Royal Academy
1770	39	Joshua Reynolds's protrait of Goldsmith exhibited at the Royal Academy. (26 May) *The Deserted Village* published by William Griffin. The poem passes through another five editions by the year's end. (July–August) Travels to Paris. Death of Mother. Writes *The Haunch of Venison*, addressed to his friend, Lord Clare
1771	40	(6 August) Publishes his *History of England*
1772	41	(20 February) Performance of his *Threnodia Augustalis*. Falls seriously ill in late summer with bladder infection
1773	42	(15 March) *She Stoops to Conquer* produced by George Colman at Covent Garden. Contributes essays to the *Westminster Magazine*

Year	Literary Context	Historical Events
1768	Death of Sterne and publication of *A Sentimental Journey Through France and Italy* First edition of the *Encyclopaedia Brittanica* (to 1771)	The Duke of Grafton becomes Prime Minister; Russo–Turkish wars (to 1792); Royal Academy founded
1769	David Garrick's Shakespeare Jubilee in Stratford-upon-Avon	John Wilkes expelled from the House of Commons amid great public agitation; James Cook's first voyage around the world (to 1770); Richard Arkwright's water-powered spinning frame patented; James Watt patents the steam engine; Royal Crescent completed at Bath; birth of Napoleon Bonaparte
1770	Birth of Wordsworth Death of Chatterton	Lord North Prime Minister (to 1782); Tea Duty instituted in American colonies; Boston Massacre
1771	Birth of Scott Mackenzie, *The Man of Feeling* Death of Smollett and publication of *The Expedition of Humphry Clinker*	
1772	Birth of Samuel Taylor Coleridge	Slavery declared untenable on English soil; Second Voyage of Captain Cook (to 1775); Kew Gardens founded
1773		Boston Tea Party protests the Tea Tax; London Stock Exchange founded

Year	Age	Life
1774	43	Comments at a meeting of The Club provoke Goldsmith to write *Retaliation*. (4 April) Dies at his lodgings in the Middle Temple from kidney disease. *Retaliation*, the *Grecian History* and the *History of the Earth, and Animated Nature* all published posthumously
1776		Monument to Goldsmith by Joseph Nollekens erected in Westminster Abbey. *The Haunch of Venison* published posthumously

Year	Literary Context	Historical Events
1774	Lord Chesterfield, *Letters*	General Election; Coercive Acts passed in response to the Boston Tea Party; First Continental Congress meets in Philadelphia; Joseph Priestly isolates oxygen
1775	Johnson, *Journey to the Western Islands of Scotland* Birth of Jane Austen	Battles of Lexington, Concord and Bunker Hill; War of American Independence (to 1783)
1776	Edward Gibbon, *Decline and Fall of the Roman Empire* (Vol. 1) Smith, *The Wealth of Nations* Bentham, *Fragment on Government* Paine, *Common Sense*	American Declaration of Independence; Third Voyage of Captain Cook (to 1780)

Introduction

In a slightly more perfect world, the reader of Oliver Goldsmith's verses would be able, upon putting down a volume of the poet's work, to turn to Samuel Johnson's complementary *Life of Goldsmith* in order to learn something more about the author. For almost fifteen years – since their first, fortuitous meeting in February 1759 – one of Goldsmith's closest friends, the Revd Thomas Percy (at the time of their first introduction Vicar of Easton-Maudit, near London and Rector of Whitby, in Northamptonshire), had jotted down notes and observations concerning his regular meetings with the writer in his diary. In time he compiled a series of documents which he decided finally to turn over to Johnson for an account of Goldsmith to be included in the latter's own monumental *Lives of the Poets* (1779–81).[1] By the time Percy passed his material on to Johnson in late 1776, his informal archives had grown to include not only his own richly anecdotal accounts of his many encounters throughout the years with 'the poor Doctor', but also a number of family letters and documents, among them an extended reminiscence of the poet's childhood written by Goldsmith's sister Catherine, and even a unique record of the author's life produced by the poet himself. Some of this same material had been given directly to Percy by Goldsmith's younger brother, Maurice, who after the poet's death in 1774 had travelled to London to see to his brother's affairs. Percy's documents, in other words, amounted to little less than a minutely chronicled narrative detailing the arc of one writer's career as it stretched through a period in the nation's literary, artistic and intellectual history. It was a period destined to be regarded by subsequent generations of English readers as an era dominated, for better or for worse, by larger-than-life figures (Johnson, Reynolds, Garrick, Burke) and characterized by a conviviality and sheer social energy which was, for lack of a better term, peculiarly 'Augustan'. Percy's authoritative collection of reminiscences and memorabilia contained the raw stuff of a grand tragi-comedy – a Grub Street epic unusually rich in its cast of supporting players – which depicted the rise to prominence of a quintessentially eighteenth-century English 'Man of Letters'.

Johnson, unfortunately, never found the time to write Goldsmith's 'Life'. His failure even to begin the project seems to have been due at least in part to the fact that the copyright on Goldsmith's most famous poem, *The Deserted Village*, did not expire until 1784 – the year of Johnson's own death – hence preventing its inclusion in any collection of verse to which the 'Life' would have formed a preface. Alternatively, as scholars such as Arthur Tillotson have argued, Johnson's own self-professed constitutional indolence may simply have prevented him from ever embarking on the work. Percy himself later opined that Johnson, who was originally to have undertaken the biography for the financial benefit of the poet's surviving relatives, in time quite simply 'forgot them and the subject'. Following Johnson's death in December 1784, his literary executor William Scott turned the material on Goldsmith over to his friend, the Shakespearian scholar Edmund Malone, who promptly returned it to Percy, who had since Goldsmith's death been promoted to the position of Bishop of Dromore. Malone suggested that Percy himself try his own hand at a 'Life' of Goldsmith. By 1786 Percy had clearly decided to do just that. A number of problems and disagreements with publishers and booksellers further delayed the appearance of Percy's memoir until 1802, when it was finally printed as the preface to a four-volume edition of Goldsmith's *Miscellaneous Works* (bearing the date 1801).

Johnson's failure to leave behind any extended account of the career of his beloved if somewhat baffling friend thus leaves Percy's *Life of Dr Oliver Goldsmith* – as one of that work's twentieth-century editors has commented – as 'the only biography of the poet written by a contemporary which can make any claim to accuracy and reliable judgements'.[2] The reliability and genuine affection of Percy's account notwithstanding, the modern reader cannot help but wish that there were other contemporary biographies either to corroborate or to contradict its author. (The *quondam* actor Samuel Glover's 1774 *Life of Goldsmith* is slight and inadequate; the accounts of the author by friends and acquaintances such as Sir Joshua Reynolds [1776], Samuel Foote [1777] and Edmund Malone [1780] are likewise valuable but sketchy and incomplete, and Boswell's references to the poet in his *Life of Johnson* are notoriously biased and unsympathetic.) Perhaps more than any other writer in the English tradition, Goldsmith stood in need of a discriminating and perceptive contemporary chronicler – one who, as Johnson himself put in his essay on the subject of biography in his *Rambler* No. 60 (1750), would have been able accurately to relate those 'incidents which give excellence to biography [which] are of a volatile and evanescent kind, such as soon escape the memory, and are rarely transmitted by tradition'. In death, as in life, Goldsmith had no such luck. Assembling a collection of historically diverse critical observations and judgements on the poet some two decades ago, G. S. Rousseau summed up the difficulty which still very much besets any reader of Goldsmith's work:

> At the heart of the problem – and it *is* a problem – lies Goldsmith's life. Virtually every critic believed it was tragic and wished to pause, ponder, and meditate on this tragedy. Poor and rich alternately, a victim of booksellers and jealous rivals, and dead by the tender age of about forty-four, Goldsmith-the-man has interested critics more than Goldsmith-the-writer. And authors writing about Goldsmith have deemed it necessary to commiserate with his sufferings, to weep for his untimely demise, and to shed a tear in his memory. Upon regaining their composure and dismissing their nostalgia, these very critics have attacked Goldsmith for not writing more prolifically, for indulging so heavily in ephemeral writing and periodical literature, and for not pursuing his greatest forte, poetry. Goldsmith's critical heritage thus displays a truly schizoid nature: his critics have been overly sentimental about his *life* . . . and unrealistically harsh about his *writings*.[3]

A sound contemporary biography of Goldsmith might at least have helped to forestall the patterns of critical response fashioned by this 'schizoid' heritage. The only real alternative to the well-established impulse of lamenting the man while condemning the body of his work – an alternative best captured in William Thackeray's description of Goldsmith as 'the most beloved of English writers' if only because our love for him is 'half pity' – was equally drastic and partial. Our unmastering sympathy for the writer's sufferings in life, according to Thackery, induces us tearfully to welcome both he and his writings into our homes and into our hearts. 'Who could harm this kind vagrant harper?' Thackeray memorably asked his readers with mawkish sentimentality in his consideration of *English*

Humourists of the Eighteenth Century (1853). 'Whom did he ever hurt?'

There is no denying that there is much material in Percy's *Life* without which our picture of Goldsmith – and, indeed, our picture of the wonderfully creative and convivial social and literary circles within which he travelled later in life – would be considerably impoverished. Recounting, for example, the preparations surrounding one of the very first encounters between Goldsmith and the 'great Lexicographer' Samuel Johnson himself, which occurred at a literary supper party at Goldsmith's lodgings in May 1761, Percy offers his own eye-witness observations in an account written in the third person. 'As they went together', he writes,

> the former [Percy himself] was much struck with the studied neatness of Johnson's dress: he had on a new suit of cloaths, a new wig nicely powdered, and every thing about him so perfectly dissimilar from his usual habits and appearance, that his companion could not help inquiring the cause of this singular transformation. 'Why, sir,' said Johnson, 'I hear that Goldsmith, who is a very great sloven, justifies his disregard of cleanliness and decency, by quoting my practice, and I am desirous this night to show him a better example.'[4]

Percy's anecdote nicely and economically captures something of the characters of both men. Johnson's confrontational sartorial rectitude was no doubt nicely balanced on the evening in question by a stubborn determination on the part of Goldsmith not to notice anything unusual about Johnson's punctilious dress at all, and a sullen refusal to comment that there was anything out of the ordinary about his unaccustomed 'neatness'. Despite their sincere friendship in later years, neither Johnson or Goldsmith would ever forget the circumstances of that early meeting. Years later, in the course of another dinner party hosted by James Boswell at his lodgings in Old Bond Street, the two would have another run-in on the subject of dress and clothing. Johnson suggested that Goldsmith's tailor had taken advantage of the poet's ridiculous vanity by fashioning for him a brightly coloured coat only in order to advertise the fact that 'he could make a coat even of so absurd a color'. The complicated and extended relationship between Johnson and Goldsmith was one characterized (at least on the part of Goldsmith) by a persistent sense of competition, rivalry and one-upmanship, all oddly tempered by a deep admiration and respect.

Percy manages neatly to establish for his readers the dominant note of the pair's friendship before the two men – at least in the historical time and place of his account – have even set eyes on one another.

For all the insight afforded by such amusing anecdotes, G. S. Rousseau's further comments on Goldsmith's critical heritage highlight the fact that Percy himself was clearly only the first of many critics and biographers to have trouble reconciling the undeniably stunning fecundity and adaptability of the poet's literary genius and talents with what could only be described as his (apparently severe and obtrusive) qualifying drawbacks of character and personality. As Johnson himself once commented of Goldsmith, 'No man was more foolish when he had not a pen in his hand, or more wise when he had.' Or as he put it on another occasion: 'If nobody was suffered to abuse poor Goldy but those who could write as well, he would have few censors.' Goldsmith's well-documented personal follies – his brash and 'clownish' behaviour – have received far more attention than those of any writer of comparable stature in our tradition. He was ridiculed throughout his own lifetime (both by his supposed friends and his enemies alike) for his 'absurdity', his 'vanity', his naïveté, his embarrassing tendency of calling a jealous attention to his own achievements, his inability to hear anyone's talents praised above his own – his general insistence on being at all times and in all companies the centre of attention. Even his appearance was ridiculed. When, in April 1770, Goldsmith's friend Sir Joshua Reynolds publicly exhibited his portrait of the writer at the Royal Academy, the painter's sister Frances could not help but comment that while the work bore more than an adequate resemblance to the Doctor himself, it was nevertheless 'the most flattering portrait she ever knew her brother to have painted'. Many biographies of Goldsmith seem at times hard pressed to say anything positive about his personality at all, and consequently appear to dwell with indecorous glee on the poet's supposed social shortcomings and *faux pas.* (The short biographical account prefaced to a selection of Goldsmith's work in one introduction to eighteenth-century literature popular among students reads more like a scathing indictment of the poet's character than a balanced introduction to his achievements as a writer.) Ralph Wardle, who produced one of the only extended and truly sympathetic biographies of Goldsmith to appear in the latter half of the twentieth century,[5] was forced by this heritage of abuse to spend the entire opening chapter of his own work defending what Hester Thrale once described as Goldsmith's 'anomalous character', and attempting to offer in its stead some convincing psychological and quite frankly social explanations for what he saw to be a fundamental misreading of the Doctor's character and motives. (That fact that Goldsmith was an Irishman and possessed an Irishman's knack for introducing a peculiarly Celtic brand of vibrant and often cryptic and self-deprecating verbal play into the conversations of his overwhelmingly serious-minded – not to say stuffy – English companions, should not be forgotten when considering the many accounts of his life.) For all such attempts at a sympathetic reading of Goldsmith's life and work, Roger Lonsdale's lament first given voice in the late 1970s remains substantially true to this day: Goldsmith still remains 'the most elusive person in the otherwise voluminously documented Johnson circle, no less a paradox to the modern biographer than he appears to have been to his contemporaries'.[6] The more one learns about Goldsmith's life, the more one is impressed by the poet's continued ability somehow to transmute the experience of suffering and tribulation into understanding and enlightening, to transform and ultimately to reconcile the stuff of individual and even national tragedy within the over-arching structure of an at times divine – and at best a *genially* divine – comedy.[7]

Born in County Westmeath to poor but respectable parents (his father was an Anglican clergyman), Goldsmith's earliest years were spent in the rural country surrounding the small village of Lissoy. Although as a boy he was one of several children, none of his four brothers were very close to him in age, and the few recollections he ever offered concerning the earliest years of his life suggest that he probably spent a great deal of time on his own. Goldsmith was to some degree a lonely and even solitary child, and like many such children he developed a remarkable sense of self-sufficiency and, some might argue, conceit. He was educated away from home, first at the Diocesan School at Elphin, then at a small institution kept by the Revd Mr Campbell at Athlone, and finally at a school at Edgeworthtown in County Longford, which was then under the direction of an old friend and colleague of his father's. A life spent almost entirely in the company of one's mother and pre-adolescent peers can be a trial for the most personable and socially confident of boys, and Goldsmith's uncertain temperament and undeniably homely appearance ('he really cut an ugly figure', his sister once recalled uncharitably) at times no doubt made those years trying ones. He finally moved on to Trinity College, Dublin (his father's *alma mater*), but his family's reduced circumstances dictated that he enter university not as a pensioner, but as a sizar – one whose fees were paid for by waiting on tables and generally acting as a servant to the other students. Needless to say, the experience was a socially demeaning one and the combination of his ungainly features and the academic dress peculiar to his 'class' of students singled Goldsmith out for constant work and even abuse. He tried his best to compensate by developing a boisterous, abrasive and self-consciously 'carefree' sense of humour, but circumstances were often against him. He considered his college tutor to be brutal and sadistic (later in life he even went so far as to characterize him as 'depraved') and could seem to muster only the slightest interest in his studies. The death of his father early in 1747 rendered his financial situation even more precarious. He was publicly admonished for taking part in an inconsequential college riot soon after learning of his father's death. He eventually satisfied his examiners and received his Bachelor's degree in 1750.

In the years immediately following his graduation, Goldsmith entertained what we would today call a number of possible 'career options'. Only nineteen yeas old, he was clearly undecided as to just how he wished to spend the rest of his life. Having first failed to obtain ordination in the Church, he was engaged for a short time as tutor with a family in County Roscommon, a post he appears to have held for just one year. Intending on one occasion to emigrate to America, Goldsmith made it only to Cork, where he managed within weeks to fritter his small savings away while waiting for the winds to shift in favour of the ship on which he had planned to engage his passage. A similar scheme, which envisioned him studying Law at the Temple in London, again saw him make it only as far as Dublin, where he similarly gambled away the fifty pounds which had been given to him by his uncle Contarine to pursue the profession. In September 1752 Goldsmith finally succeeded in leaving Ireland. He headed for Scotland, where he entered the University of Edinburgh to study medicine. Within less than two years he had again moved on, this time to Holland to continue his medical studies at Leyden University. At both institutions he was constantly short of money and complained to his uncle and benefactor that even the most necessary of provisions were 'extreamly Dear'. Ostensibly contemplating the further continuation of his medical studies by attending lectures at the Sorbonne in Paris, Goldsmith headed south towards the French capital in the late winter of 1755. His wanderings across the Continent, accomplished largely on foot, led him in time through France to Switzerland, Germany and even Italy. He did not return to the United Kingdom until February 1756.

Having decided to settle for the time being in London, Goldsmith characteristically made little practical use of his medical training. He only half-heartedly pursued the profession for which he had trained so many years, working first as an assistant to an apothecary and subsequently as a physician in Bankside, in Southwark, London. The same period saw him engaged as well as a proof-reader in the printing house run by the novelist Samuel Richardson, and even as an usher at a Presbyterian boys' school in Surrey. In the spring of 1757 he was introduced to Ralph Griffiths, a bookseller and editor of the popular *Monthly Review*, who recognized in Goldsmith a man whose learning and experience would suit him to the position of a reviewer and essayist for the *Monthly*. Within days of their meeting, Goldsmith was installed in a set of rooms above Griffiths's shop in Paternoster Row, near St Paul's Cathedral, and his career as a hack writer and journalist had begun.

Goldsmith at first contented himself with reviewing books (one issue of the *Monthly* finds him contributing no less than twenty-seven notices on recent publications) and offering his own translations of the work of French authors such as Jean Marteilhe's *Mémoires d'un Protestant*. Yet Griffiths's publication was to prove for Goldsmith only a convenient starting point. The next few years saw the Doctor (as he was soon commonly known) writing for a wide range of popular periodicals, including the *Busy Body*, the *Weekly Magazine*, the *British Magazine* and Tobias Smollett's *Critical Review*. Goldsmith's own periodical, *The Bee*, appeared in October and November 1759, the same year which had earlier witnessed the publication of his first substantial work, *An Enquiry into the Present State of Learning in Europe*. Goldsmith's career as a writer was reasonably secure by 1760, when he began contributing his series of 'Chinese Letters' to John Newbery's *Public Ledger*. The 'Letters', which pretended to view the habits and customs of the English nation through the eyes of a foreigner, would be collected and republished as *The Citizen of the World* in 1762. Works like the *Enquiry*, *The Bee* and the 'Chinese Letters' served at least to bring Goldsmith to the attention of individuals such Edmund Burke, Edward Young and Johnson, and the Doctor soon found himself on familiar terms with the most impressive and influential individuals in the London publishing world. Despite many differences in temperament and habit, Johnson would, again, in time become one of Goldsmith's most outspoken champions and supporters. Together with Joshua Reynolds and David Garrick, Johnson and Goldsmith in 1763 formed the famous Literary 'Club' which met informally at the Turk's Head, in Soho, to discuss matters of contemporary taste in literature, drama and criticism. *The Traveller, or, A Prospect of Society*, a poem based in part on Goldsmith's own wanderings on the Continent in 1755, was published on 19 December 1764 to considerable popular acclaim. Eight more editions of the poem were to appear in Goldsmith's lifetime. Goldsmith, who once famously complained about his neglect as a writer by observing that whenever he published anything, 'the publick make a point to know nothing about it', had by the earliest months of 1765 finally found himself a well-known and – in some circles – even respected man.

For all his comparative success as a writer, however, Goldsmith seemed incapable of keeping his head above water financially. At such practical matters he was hopeless, and the story of the manner in which his sentimental novel *The Vicar of Wakefield* was only indirectly and almost by accident sold for publication owing to its author's straitened circumstances is well known even to this day, thanks largely to Boswell's 'exact narration' in his *Life of Johnson* of Johnson's own vividly anecdotal account of the transaction. 'I received one morning a message from poor Goldsmith that he was in great distress,' Johnson recalled,

and, as it was not in his power to come to me, begging that I would come to him as soon as possible. I sent him a guinea, and promised to come to him directly. I accordingly went as soon as I was drest, and found that his landlady had arrested him for his rent, at which he was in a violent passion. I perceived that he had already changed my guinea, and had got a bottle of Madeira and a glass before him. I put the cork in the bottle, desired he would be calm, and began to talk to him of the means by which he might be extricated. He then told me that he had a novel ready for the press, which he produced to me. I looked into it, and saw its merit: told the landlady I should soon return, and having gone to a bookseller, sold it for sixty pounds. I brought Goldsmith the money, and he discharged his rent, not without rating his landlady in a high tone for having used him so ill.[8]

The Vicar of Wakefield was not published until March 1766, some two and a half years after the rather embarrassing anecdote related by Johnson had taken place. The comparative success of the novel (it passed through three editions in six months, and continued to increase in popularity throughout the remainder of its author's life) failed, however, to alleviate in any way Goldsmith's tenuous financial existence. He had, after all, sold his rights to its profits and at the time had no real project in mind with which to follow its success. Looking to find a more lucrative means of displaying his talents, Goldsmith in 1767 decided to try his hand writing for the stage. The result was his gentle satire on the current vogue for what was then known as 'sentimental' (as opposed to 'laughing') comedy, *The Good Natured Man*. The play premiered early the following year at London's Covent Garden, where it enjoyed a respectable but by no means spectacular run of ten nights (Goldsmith earned some four hundred pounds from the three performances which were specifically for the author's benefit). Goldsmith's second attempt at a theatrical comedy would be *She Stoops to Conquer* (1773), which was likewise to be produced by George Colman at Covent Garden. This second comedy was an overwhelming popular success (running twelve nights in its first season and soon revived), and secured its author an immediate reward of over five hundred pounds.

Even three years before the success of *She Stoops to Conquer*, however, Goldsmith's talents as a poet and creative writer in general had finally been more fully recognized by the public when William Griffin published his *The Deserted Village* in a handsome quarto edition. A sentimental lament for the depopulation of the country and a condemnation of the consecration of 'luxury' as 'one of the greatest national advantages', *The Deserted Village* struck a sympathetic nerve among a broad range of English readers, who for years responded to the poem's simple nostalgia and praise of rural life with genuine emotion and, for all the poem's (supposed) anachronisms, apparent recognition. Much like Thomas Gray's

Elegy Written in a Country Churchyard (1751), Goldsmith's pastoral elegy was praised for its clarity, its simplicity of diction and expression, and for what Ralph Wardle has called its 'elemental appeal'. *The Deserted Village* passed through six editions in the course of less than one year, and was very soon being translated into French, German and Italian. The work remains to this day one of the most frequently anthologized poems in the English language.

Goldsmith was unfortunately not allowed to enjoy the fruits of his success either as a poet or a dramatist for very long. Still flush with the critical acclaim and the substantial profits which greeted *She Stoops to Conquer* in the spring and early summer of 1773, Goldsmith was hard at work on a number of unfinished commissions – including a multi-volume *Grecian History*, an abridgement of his 1771 *History of England* and the ambitiously titled *History of the Earth, and Animated Nature* – when he succumbed to a series of severe and painful attacks of kidney trouble. His own training as a physican no doubt warning him that the end was near, Goldsmith died while seized with the violent convulsions of one such attack at his residence in London's Temple on 4 April 1774. His last major poem, the unfinished *Retaliation*, was published only weeks after its author's death.

Preparing an edition of Goldsmith's *Poems and Plays* for the Everyman's Library in 1975, the scholar Tom Davis observed that all of Goldsmith's most important poems seem to fall rather naturally into three broad categories.[8] The first of these categories – one which would include the lengthier works reprinted here, such as *The Traveller, The Deserted Village, Thredonia Augustalis* and *The Captivity* – Davis described as 'formal' and 'self-consciously serious'. Goldsmith's poems of this sort tend for the most part to be professedly 'straightforward' works, in the sense that they appear noticeably to lack any ironic perspective on or distance from their subjects. Unlike so many of their author's other productions, they pointedly eschew satire and parody. Despite their emphatically public nature, these lengthier verses could nevertheless at their best – as works such as *The Traveller* so clearly demonstrate – subtly and successfully depict a complex state of mind and even balance the sophisticated, individual sensibility so characteristic of the mid-century English poet against what Davis called 'the impersonal generalizing wisdom of Augustanism'. They could likewise, on the other hand, be self-confessed hack work (e.g. *Threnodia Augustalis*), reflecting what one rather reluctantly admits to be some of the weakest qualities of eighteenth-century verse, and standing so close to generic self-parody as almost to necessitate a headnote alerting readers to their genuine seriousness of purpose.

The Traveller and *The Deserted Village* stand head and shoulders above Goldsmith's other poems in this first category. Bear in mind, however, that even these two works have necessarily risen and fallen in critical estimation over the years (*The Deserted Village*, for example, was largely reviled by nineteenth-century critics – most notably Macaulay – on both aesthetic and political grounds, and neither that poem nor its predecessor attracted much of the attention lavished by the New Critics of the 1930s and 1940s on works of similar length by authors, e.g. Gray, Collins, Crabbe, from roughly the same historical period). *The Traveller* – which Johnson grandly deemed the finest poem to be produced by an Englishman since the death of Pope – is a 'prospect' poem which scans the European continent and offers its readers a comparative study of the national temperaments of the several countries (Italy, Switzerland, France, Holland, Britain) which fall within the purview of the melancholy wanderer whose Alpine observations it pretends to offer to the reader. The inhabitants of each nation are said to be blessed with peculiar (and, one is led to suppose, geographically, racially and demographically precise) advantages. The French, for example, exhibit a pleasing 'mirth and social ease' which some might consider the envy of their hard-working and often dour neighbours, but that same national constitution or genius tends likewise to encourage an enfeebling and effeminate 'pride' and ostentation. Likewise the British are the fortunate heirs to a strong and unique tradition of freedom and independence, but that same freedom can in turn lead to a factious arrogance of spirit which, given free reign, threatens to '[break] the social tie'. The observer, who looks at the beginning of the poem from within his own isolation and exile to find 'the happiest spot' on earth, is left at the poem's end with the conviction that such terrestrial happiness can paradoxically exist only 'in the mind'. 'Our own felicity', the poem finally declares, 'we make or find'. For all the vaguely xenophobic humour of the poem's description and for all the Christian stoicism of its fundamental message, the world of *The Traveller* is a surprisingly dark and inhospitable place in which, as the critic Eric Rothstein has put it, the careworn individual observer faces an overwhelming universe 'about which he can do little.' No doubt part of the essential brilliance of the poem, as Rothstein goes on to comment, lies in the manner in which the work's own concessive rhetorical structure, whereby 'the repairing of one evil creates vulnerability to the next', mirrors and embodies this moral meaning.[9] The beneficent and divinely comedic structure of the universe ('Nature', in the poem, is still characterized as 'a mother kind alike to all') is in Goldsmith's verse epistle perhaps realized only in the possibility of retreat from the 'toil' and 'pain' of the great world, and clear only to those who realize the vain and delusory nature of human hopes and desires.

The Deserted Village reflects a moral sensibility very much similar to that first given voice in *The Traveller*. Like the earlier poem, this later, more mature work is in some respects rooted in Goldsmith's own lived experience. If *The Traveller* draws on the poet's observations while undertaking his own tour of the Continent in 1755, *The Deserted Village* relies similarly on memories of his own childhood in Lissoy. In both works Goldsmith transforms the stuff of individual memory and nostalgic, melancholy meditation into works of 'universalized' significance. The narrative of *The Deserted Village* descries the practice of destroying old and long-established country hamlets and villages in the name of agricultural progress, and enclosing and incorporating the land into the estates of the wealthy. Yet the poem focuses not so much on this condemnation of trade and 'luxury' (a condemnation which is to some degree given fuller voice in the 'Dedication' to the work rather than in the poem itself), as on its author's loving description of a rural and some would say Edenic English existence. The health and plenty, the innocence and ease of 'Sweet Auburn', however, exists only in the past. Goldsmith's poet in *The Deserted Village*, as in *The Traveller*, is once again condemned to wander the world a postlapsarian exile, whose only weapon against Fate in his quest for enlightenment is a lived understanding of what Johnson would in his own poetry characterize as 'the vanity of human wishes'.

Davis's second category for Goldsmith's poems includes humorous short works such as the 'Elegy on the Death of a Mad Dog', songs such as 'When lovely woman stoops to folly' from *The Vicar of Wakefield*, and the 'Ballad' of Edwin and Angelina from the same novel. These are examples of 'light verse' in the best sense of that tradition, and critics such as Ralph Wardle have undoubtedly been

correct to argue that even those pieces which might at first appear
to ask to be taken 'seriously' (the 'Ballad', for example), are in fact
on some level poking fun at the very sentimentality which they
would seem, when taken out of context, to embody. Much of this
shorter poetry often reminds the reader of the work of Goldsmith's
predecessors – most notably of Swift, occasionally of Pope and at
times even of Skelton – but the Doctor lacks (or softens) Swift's
sardonic anger, forsakes (to some degree) Pope's rhetorical and
syntactical precision and would probably not even have recognized
the whiplash sting of Skelton's uncontrollable fury. Goldsmith's
light verse, as William Hazlitt noted in 1824, resembles his longer
poems insofar as it seems 'spontaneous, unstudied, yet elegant,
harmonious, graceful, nearly faultless'.[10] Yet all is not, as some
critics have suggested, entirely light-hearted and inconsequential.
Poems such as *The Traveller* and *The Deserted Village* present their
readers with the image of an individual who is forced to face alone
the rigors and challenges of an ironic universe which seems to be
indifferent and at times positively hostile to his hopes and desires.
The destabilizing *bathos* of so many of Goldsmith's designedly
slighter works tends similarly to reflect the sensibility so often given
voice in Augustan satire that things – and this is a fact we choose
not to recognize at our peril – are not necessarily as they seem to be.

The final group of poems recognized by Davis are more personal,
'conversational' works. Insofar as they are genial and generally
brief verses, often addressed to close friends and never intended for
public circulation or 'mass' consumption, these works likewise
participate in a long-standing tradition of designedly self-depreca-
tory, epistolary response poetry. (One thinks, for example, of works
such as Ben Jonson's 'Inviting a Friend to Supper' – itself indebted
to the work of the Roman epigrammatist Martial – or Swift's many
verse 'Letters' to his friends and critics.) Many of these pieces are
understandable only within the context of Goldsmith's biography,
most notably the extraordinary poem he left unfinished at his
death, *Retaliation*. In this last work – a poem which Davis rather
nicely characterizes as maintaining a satiric tone of 'devastating
gentleness' – one is perhaps closer to Goldsmith the man than in
any of his other, more polished and considered works.[11] Its vantage
and its criticism, remarkable in that it exposes itself 'with some
courage to the censure of those whom it censures, demanding that
they recognize the wisdom of its praise, [and] the justice of its

attack', accomplishes the no less remarkable task of ending Goldsmith's professional career on a positively dignified note.

ROBERT L. MACK

References

1. For information on Percy's *Life* see Richard L. Harp, *Thomas Percy's Life of Dr Oliver Goldsmith*, edited with an Introduction and Notes, Salzburg Studies in English Literature, No. 52 (Salzburg: Universität Salzburg, 1976), pp. viii–xxviii.
2. Harp, *Thomas Percy's Life of Dr Oliver Goldsmith*, p. 8.
3. G. S. Rousseau, Introduction, *Goldsmith: The Criticial Heritage* (London: Routledge & Kegan Paul, 1974), p. 7.
4. Percy, *Life of Dr Oliver Goldsmith*, pp. 62–3.
5. For an extended and sympathetic account of Goldsmith's life, see Ralph M. Wardle, *Oliver Goldsmith* (Lawrence, Kansas: University of Kansas Press, 1957).
6. Roger Lonsdale, '"A Garden, and a Grave": The Poetry of Oliver Goldsmith', in *The Author in His Work: Essays on a Problem in Criticism*, eds Louis L. Martz and Aubrey Williams (New Haven, Connecticut: Yale University Press, 1978), repr. in *Oliver Goldsmith: Modern Critical Views*, ed. Harold Bloom (New York: Chelsea House, 1987), pp. 49–72.
7. James Boswell, *Life of Johnson*, ed. R. W. Chapman (Oxford: Oxford University Press, 1980), p. 294.
8. Tom Davis, ed., *Oliver Goldsmith: Poems and Plays* (London: Everyman, 1975), pp. xix–xxii.
9. See Eric Rothstein, *Restoration and Eighteenth-Century Poetry, 1660–1780* (London: Routledge & Kegan Paul, 1981), pp. 121, 140.
10. William Hazlitt, from *A Critical List of Authors from Select British Poets* (1824), repr. in G. S. Rousseau, *Goldsmith: The Critical Heritage*, p. 258.
    11. Davis, *Oliver Goldsmith: Poems and Plays*, p. xxi.

Oliver Goldsmith

On a Beautiful Youth Struck
Blind With Lightning

Sure 'twas by Providence design'd,
Rather in pity, than in hate,
That he should be, like Cupid, blind,
To save him from Narcissus' fate.

The Gift

To Iris, in Bow-Street, Covent-Garden

Say, cruel Iris, pretty rake,
    Dear mercenary beauty,
What annual offering shall I make,
    Expressive of my duty.

My heart, a victim to thine eyes,
    Should I at once deliver,
Say, would the angry fair one prize
    The gift, who slights the giver.

A bill, a jewel, watch, or toy,
    My rivals give – and let 'em.
If gems, or gold, impart a joy,
    I'll give them – when I get 'em.

I'll give – but not the full-blown rose,
    Or rose-bud more in fashion;
Such short-liv'd offerings but disclose
    A transitory passion.

I'll give thee something yet unpaid,
    Not less sincere, than civil:

I'll give thee – Ah! too charming maid;
   I'll give thee – To the Devil.   20

A Sonnet

Weeping, murmuring, complaining,
   Lost to every gay delight;
Myra, too sincere for feigning,
   Fears th' approaching bridal night.

Yet, why this killing soft dejection?
   Why dim thy beauty with a tear?
Had Myra followed my direction,
   She long had wanted cause to fear.

An Elegy
on that Glory of her Sex
Mrs Mary Blaize

Good people all, with one accord,
   Lament for Madam Blaize,
Who never wanted a good word –
   From those who spoke her praise.

The needy seldom pass'd her door,
   And always found her kind;
She freely lent to all the poor, –
   Who left a pledge behind.

She strove the neighbourhood to please,
   With manners wond'rous winning,   10

And never follow'd wicked ways, –
    Unless when she was sinning.

At church, in silks and sattins new,
    With hoop of monstrous size,
She never slumber'd in her pew, –
    But when she shut her eyes.

Her love was sought, I do aver,
    By twenty beaus and more;
The king himself has follow'd her, –
    When she has walk'd before.   20

But now her wealth and finery fled,
    Her hangers-on cut short all;
The doctors found, when she was dead, –
    Her last disorder mortal.

Let us lament, in sorrow sore,
    For Kent-Street well may say,
That had she liv'd a twelve-month more, –
    She had not dy'd today.

The Double Transformation: A Tale

Secluded from domestic strife
Jack Bookworm led a college life;
A fellowship at twenty five
Made him the happiest man alive,
He drank his glass, and crack'd his joke,
And Freshmen wonder'd as he spoke;
He rak'd and toasted, dived or shone:
And even was thought a knowing one.
Without politeness aim'd at breeding,
And laugh'd at pedantry and reading;   10

Thus sad or sober, gay or mellow,
Jack was a *college pretty fellow.*
    Such pleasures unallay'd with care,
Could any accident impair?
Could Cupid's shaft at length transfix,
Our swain arriv'd at thirty six?
O had the archer ne'er come down
To ravage in a country town!
Or Flavia been content to stop,
At triumphs in a Fleet-street shop.   20
O had her eyes forgot to blaze!
Or Jack had wanted eyes to gaze:
O – but let exclamation cease,
Her presence banish'd all his peace.
    Our altered Parson now began,
To be a perfect ladies man;
Made sonnets, lisp'd his sermons o'er,
And told the tales he told before,
Of bailiffs pump'd, and proctors bit,
At college how he shew'd his wit;   30
And as the fair one still approv'd,
He fell in love – or thought he lov'd.
    They laugh'd, they talk'd with giddy glee,
Miss had her jokes as well as he:
In short, their love was passing wonder,
They tallied as if torn assunder;
So with decorum all things carried,
Miss frown'd, and blush'd, and then was – married.
    Need we expose to vulgar sight,
The raptures of the bridal night?   40
Need we intrude on hallow'd ground,
Or draw the curtains clos'd around:
Let it suffice, that each had charms,
He clasp'd a goddess in his arms;
And tho' she felt his usage rough,
Yet in a man 'twas well enough.
    And here discretion might prevail,
To interrupt the tedious tale;
Poetic justice bids it rest,

And leave 'em both completely blest: 50
Yet more importunate than they,
Truth bids me on, and I obey.
    The honeymoon like lightening flew,
The second brought its transports too.
A third, a fourth were not amiss,
The fifth was friendship mix'd with bliss:
But when a twelvemonth pass'd away
Jack found his goddess made of clay:
Found half the charms that deck'd her face,
Arose from powder, shreds or lace;   60
But still the worst remain'd behind,
That very face had rob'd her mind.
    Skill'd in no other arts was she,
But dressing, patching, repartee;
And just as humour rose or fell,
By turns a slattern or a belle:
'Tis true she dress'd with modern grace,
Half naked at a ball or race;
But when at home, at board or bed,
Five greasy nightcaps wrap'd her head: 70
Could so much beauty condescend,
To be a dull domestic friend?
Could any courtain lectures bring,
To decency so fine a thing?
In short by night 'twas fits or fretting,
By day 'twas gadding or coquetting.
Fond to be seen she kept a bevy,
Of powder'd coxcombs at her levy;
The squire and captain took their stations,
And twenty other near relations;   80
Jack suck'd his pipe and often broke
A sigh in suffocating smoke;
She in her turn became perplexing,
And found substantial bliss in vexing.
While all their hours were pass'd between
Insulting repartee or spleen:

Thus as her faults each day were known,
He thinks her features coarser grown;
He fancies every vice she shews,
Or thins her lip, or points her nose: 90
Whenever rage or envy rise,
How wide her mouth, how wild her eyes!
He knows not how, but so it is,
Her face is grown a knowing phyz;
And tho' her fops are wondrous civil,
He thinks her ugly as the Devil.

Now to perplex the ravell'd nooze,
As each a different way pursues,
While sullen or loquacious strife,
Promis'd to hold them on for life,   100
That dire disease whose ruthless power
Withers the beauty's transient flower:
Lo! the small pox with horrid glare,
Levell'd its terrors at the fair;
And rifling every youthful grace,
Left but the remnant of a face.

The glass grown hateful to her sight,
Reflected now a perfect fright:
Each former art she vainly tries
To bring back lustre to her eyes.   110
In vain she tries her pastes and creams,
To smooth her skin, or hide its seams;
Her country beaux and city cousins,
Lovers no more; flew off by dozens:
The squire himself was seen to yield,
And even the captain quit the field.

Poor Madam now condemn'd to hack
The rest of life with anxious Jack,
Perceiving others fairly flown
Attempted pleasing him alone.   120
Jack soon was dazzl'd to behold
Her present face surpass the old;
With modesty her cheeks are dy'd,
Humility displaces pride;

For tawdry finery is seen,
A person ever neatly clean:
No more presuming on her sway
She learns good nature every day,
Serenely gay, and strict in duty,
Jack finds his wife a perfect beauty.   130

Description of an Author's Bed-Chamber

Where the Red Lion flaring o'er the way,
Invites each passing stranger that can pay;
Where Calvert's butt, and Parson's black champaign,
Regale the drabs and bloods of Drury lane;
There in a lonely room, from bailiffs snug,
The muse found Scroggen stretch'd beneath a rug,
A window patch'd with paper lent a ray,
That dimly shew'd the state in which he lay;
The sanded floor that grits beneath the tread;
The humid wall with paltry pictures spread: 10
The royal game of goose was there in view,
And the twelve rules the royal martyr drew;
The seasons fram'd with listing found a place,
And brave prince William shew'd his lamp-black face:
The morn was cold, he views with keen desire
The rusty grate unconscious of a fire:
With beer and milk arrears the frieze was scor'd,
And five crack'd tea cups dress'd the chimney board.
A night-cap deck'd his brows instead of bay,
A cap by night – a stocking all the day!   20

On Seeing Mrs ****, Perform in the Character of ****

To you bright fair the nine address their lays,
And tune my feeble voice to sing thy praise.
The heart-felt power of every charm divine,
Who can withstand their all-commanding shine?
See how she moves along with every grace
While soul-brought tears steal down each shining face,
She speaks, 'tis rapture all and nameless bliss,
Ye gods what transport e'er compar'd to this.
As when in Paphian groves the queen of love,
With fond complaint address'd the listening Jove,   10
'Twas joy, and endless blisses all around,
And rocks forgot their hardness at the sound.
Then first, at last even Jove was taken in,
And felt here charms, without disguise, within.

On the Death of the Right Honourable ***

Ye muses, pour the pitying tear
For Pollio snatch'd away:
O had he liv'd another year!
– *He had not dy'd today.*

O, were he born to bless mankind,
In virtuous times of yore,
Heroes themselves had fallen behind!
– *Whene'er he went before.*

How sad the groves and plains appear,
And sympathetic sheep: 10

Even pitying hills would drop a tear!
— *If hills could learn to weep.*

His bounty is exalted strain
Each bard might well display:
Since none implor'd relief in vain!
— *That went reliev'd away.*

And hark! I hear the tuneful throng
His obsequies forbid.
He still shall live, shall live as long
— *As ever dead man did.*   20

An Elegy on the Death of a Mad Dog

Good people all, of every sort,
    Give ear unto my song;
And if you find it wond'rous short,
    It cannot hold you long.

In Isling town there was a man,
    Of whom the world might say,
That still a godly race he ran,
    Whene'er he went to pray.

A kind and gentle heart he had,
    To comfort friends and foes;   10
The naked every day he clad,
    When he put on his cloaths.

And in that town a dog was found,
    As many dogs there be,
Both mungrel, puppy, whelp, and hound,
    And curs of low degree.

This dog and man at first were friends;
    But when a pique began,
The dog, to gain some private ends,
    Went mad and bit the man.   20

Around from all the neighbouring streets,
    The wondering neighbours ran,
And swore the dog had lost his wits,
    To bite so good a man.

The wound it seem'd both sore and sad,
    To every christian eye;
And while they swore the dog was mad,
    They swore the man would die.

But soon a wonder came to light,
    That shew'd the rogues they lied,   30
The man recovered of the bite,
    The dog it was that dy'd.

Song From *The Vicar of Wakefield*

When lovely woman stoops to folly,
    And finds too late that men betray,
What charm can sooth her melancholy,
    What art can wash her guilt away?

The only art her guilt to cover,
    To hide her shame from every eye,
To give repentance to her lover,
And wring his bosom – is to die.

Edwin and Angelina:
A Ballad

Turn, gentle hermit of the dale,
  And guide my lonely way,
To where yon taper cheers the vale,
  With hospitable ray.

For here forlorn and lost I tread,
  With fainting steps and slow;
Where wilds immeasurably spread,
  Seem lengthening as I go.

'Forbear, my son,' the hermit cries,
  'To tempt the dangerous gloom;   10
For yonder faithless phantom flies
  To lure thee to thy doom.

Here to the houseless child of want,
  My door is open still;
And tho' my portion is but scant,
  I give it with good will.

Then turn tonight, and freely share
  Whate'er my cell bestows;
My rushy couch, and frugal fare,
  My blessing and repose.   20

No flocks that range the valley free,
  To slaughter I condemn:
Taught by that power that pities me,
  I learn to pity them.

But from the mountain's grassy side,
  A guiltless feast I bring;
A scrip with herbs and fruits supply'd,
  And water from the spring.

Then, pilgrim, turn, thy cares forego;
    All earth-born cares are wrong: 30
'Man wants but little here below,
    Nor wants that little long.'

Soft as the dew from heav'n descends,
    His gentle accents fell:
The modest stranger lowly bends,
    And follows to the cell.

Far in a wilderness obscure
    The lonely mansion lay;
A refuge to the neighbouring poor,
    And strangers led astray.   40

No stores beneath its humble thatch
    Requir'd a master's care;
The wicket opening with a latch,
    Receiv'd the harmless pair.

And now when busy crowds retire
    To take their evening rest,
The hermit trimm'd his little fire,
    And cheer'd his pensive guest:

And spread his vegetable store,
    And gayly prest, and smil'd;   50
And skill'd in legendary lore,
    The lingering hours beguil'd.

Around in sympathetic mirth
    Its tricks the kitten tries,
The cricket chirrups in the hearth;
    The crackling faggot flies.

But nothing could a charm import
    To sooth the stranger's woe:
For grief was heavy at his heart,
    And tears began to flow.   60

His rising cares the hermit spy'd,
   With answering care opprest:
'And whence, unhappy youth,' he cry'd,
   'The sorrows of thy breast?

From better habitations spurn'd,
   Reluctant dost thou rove;
Or grieve for friendship unreturn'd,
   Or unregarded love?

Alas! the joys that fortune brings,
   Are trifling and decay;   70
And those who prize the paltry things,
   More trifling still than they.

And what is friendship but a name,
   A charm that lulls to sleep;
A shade that follows wealth or fame,
   But leaves the wretch to weep?

And love has still an emptier sound,
   The modern fair one's jest:
On earth unseen, or only found
   To warm the turtle's nest.   80

For shame fond youth thy sorrows hush,
   And spurn the sex,' he said:
But while he spoke a rising blush
   His love-lorn guest betray'd.

Surpriz'd he sees new beauties rise,
   Swift mantling to the view;
Like colours o'er the morning skies,
   As bright, as transient too.

The bashful look, the rising breast,
   Alternate spread alarms: 90

The lovely stranger stands confest
   A maid in all her charms.

'And, ah, forgive a stranger rude,
   A wretch forlorn,' she cry'd;
'Whose feet unhallowed thus intrude
   Where heaven and you reside.

But let a maid thy pity share,
   Whom love has taught to stray;
Who seeks for rest, but finds despair
   Companion of her way.   100

My father liv'd beside the Tyne,
   A wealthy Lord was he;
And all his wealth was mark'd as mine,
   He had but only me.

To win me from his tender arms,
   Unnumber'd suitors came;
Who prais'd me for imputed charms,
   And felt or feign'd a flame.

Each hour a mercenary crowd,
   With richest proffers strove: 110
Among the rest young Edwin bow'd,
   But never talk'd of love.

In humble simplest habit clad,
   No wealth nor power had he;
Wisdom and worth were all he had,
   But these were all to me.

The blossom opening to the day,
   The dews of heaven refin'd,
Could nought of purity display,
   To emulate his mind.   120

The dew, the blossom on the tree,
　　With charms inconstant shine;
Their charms were his, but woe to me,
　　Their constancy was mine.

For still I try'd each fickle art,
　　Importunate and vain;
And while his passion touch'd my heart,
　　I triumph'd in his pain.

Till quite dejected with my scorn,
　　He left me to my pride;   130
And sought a solitude forlorn,
　　In secret where he died.

But mine the sorrow, mine the fault,
　　And well my life shall pay;
I'll seek the solitude he sought,
　　And stretch me where he lay.

And there forlorn despairing hid,
　　I'll lay me down and die:
'Twas so for me that Edwin did,
　　And so for him will I.'   140

'Forbid it heaven!' the hermit cry'd,
　　And clasp'd her to his breast:
The wondering fair one turn'd to chide,
　　'Twas Edwin's self that prest.

'Turn, Angelina, ever dear,
　　My charmer, turn to see,
Thy own, thy long-lost Edwin here,
　　Restor'd to love and thee.

Thus let me hold thee to my heart,
　　And ev'ry care resign: 150
And shall we never, never part,
　　My life – my all that's mine.

No, never, from this hour to part,
   We'll live and love so true;
The sigh that rends thy constant heart,
   Shall break thy Edwin's too.'

The Captivity: An Oratorio

Act I Scene I

Israelites sitting on the Banks of the Euphrates

1st Prophet

Recitativo

Ye Captive tribes that hourly work and weep
Where flows Euphrates murmuring to the deep,
Suspend a while the task, the tear suspend,
And turn to God your father and your friend:
Insulted, chaind, and all the world a foe,
Our God alone is all we boast below.

Chorus of Israelites

Our God is all we boast below:
To him we turn our eyes,
And every added weight of woe
Shall make our homage rise;   10

And tho' no temple richly drest
Nor sacrifice is here,
Wee'l make his temple in our breast
And offer up a tear.

2nd Prophet

Recitative

That strain once more, it bids remembrance rise,
And calls my long lost country to mine eyes.
Ye fields of Sharon, drest in flowery pride,
Ye Plains where Jordan rolls its glassy tide,
Ye hills of Lebanon with cedars crownd,
Ye Gilead groves that fling perfumes around;   20
These hills how sweet, those plains how wondrous fair,
But sweeter still when heaven was with us there.

Air

O memory thou fond deceiver,
Still importunate and vain,
To former joys recurring ever,
And turning all the past to pain:

Hence deceiver most distressing,
Seek the happy and the free,
They who want each other blessing
Ever want a friend in thee.   30

1st Prophet

Recitativo

Yet, why repine? What tho' by bonds confind,
Should bonds enslave the vigour of the mind?
Have we not cause for triumph when we see
Ourselves alone from idol worship free?
Are not this very day those rites begun
Where prostrate folly hails the rising sun?
Do not our tyrant Lords this day ordain
For superstition's rites and mirth profane?
And should we mourn? Should coward virtue fly
When impious folly rears her front on high?   40
No, rather let us triumph still the more
And as our fortune sinks our wishes soar.

Air

The triumphs that on vice attend
Shall ever in confusion end;
The good man suffers but to gain
And every virtue springs from pain;

As Aromatic plants bestow
No spicy fragrance while they grow,
But crush'd or trodden to the ground
Diffuse their balmy sweets around.   50

2nd Prophet

Recitative

But hush, my sons, our tyrant Lords are near;
The sound of barbarous mirth offends mine ear.
Triumphant music floats along the vale:
Near, nearer still, it gathers on the gale;
The growing note their near approach declares:
Desist my sons, nor mix the strain with theirs.

Enter Chaldean Priests attended

1st Priest

Air

Come on, my companions, the triumph display:
Let rapture the minutes employ,
The sun calls us out on this festival day,
And our monarch partakes of our Joy.   60

Like the sun our great monarch all pleasure supplies;
Both similar blessings bestow:
The sun with his splendour illumines the skies,
And our Monarch enlivens below.

Chaldean Woman

Air

Haste, ye sprightly sons of pleasure,
Love presents its brightest treasure,
Leave all other sports for me.

Chaldean Attendant

Or rather, loves delights despising,
Haste to raptures ever rising,
Wine shall bless the brave and free.   70

2nd Priest

Wine and beauty thus inviting,
Each to different joys exciting,
Whither shall my choice encline?

1st Priest

I'll waste no longer in chusing,
But, neither love nor wine refusing,
I'll make them both together mine.

Recitative

But whence, when joy should brighten oer the land,
This sullen gloom in Judah's Captive band?
Ye sons of Judah, why the lute unstrung,
Or why those harps on yonder willows hung?   80
Come, leave your griefs, and Join our warbling Choir:
For who like you can wake the sleeping lyre?

2nd Prophet

Bow'd down with Chains, the scorn of all mankind,
To Want, to toil, and every ill consign'd;
Is this a time to bid us raise the strain
And mix in rites that heaven regards with pain?
No, never; may this hand forget each art
That speeds the powers of music to the heart,
Ere I forget the land that gave me birth,
Or Join with sounds profane its sacred mirth.   90

1st Priest

Insulting slaves, if gentler methods fail,
The whips and angry tortures shall prevail.

Exeunt Chaldeans

1st Prophet

Why, let them come, one good remains to cheer:
We fear the Lord, and know no other fear.

Chorus

Can whips or tortures hurt the mind
On God's supporting breast reclind?
Stand fast and let our tyrants see
That fortitude is Victory.

End of the first Act

Act II

Scene as Before

Chorus of Israelites

O Peace of mind, thou lovely guest,
Thou softest soother of the breast,   100
Dispense thy balmy store;
Wing all our thoughts to reach the skies,
Till earth, diminish'd to our eyes,
Shall vanish as we soar.

1st Priest

Recitative

No more, too long has justice been delay'd,
The king's commands must fully be obey'd;
Compliance with his will your peace secures:
Praise but our Gods, and every good is yours.
But if, rebellious to his high command,

You spurn the favours offer'd from his hand,   110
Think timely, think what ills remain behind:
Reflect, nor tempt to rage the royal mind.

2nd Priest

Air

Fierce is the whirlwind howling
Oer Afric's sandy plain
And Fierce the tempest rolling
Along the furrow'd main.

But storms that fly
To rend the sky,
Every ill presaging,
Less dreadful shew   120
To worlds below
Than angry monarchs raging.

Israelitish Woman

Recitative

Ah me! what angry terrors round us grow,
How shrinks my soul to meet the threaten'd blow;
Ye Prophets, skilld in heaven's eternal truth,
Forgive my sexe's fears, forgive my youth,
If shrinking thus when frowning power appears
I wish for life, and yield me to my fears.
Let us one hour, one little hour, obey;
Tomorrows tears may wash our stains away.   130

Air

To the last moment of his breath
On hope the wretch relies,
And even the pang preceding death
Bids Expectation rise.

Hope like the gleaming taper's light
Adorns and cheers our way,

And still, as darker grows the night,
Emits a brighter ray.

2nd Priest

Recitative

Why this delay? at length for joy prepare;
I read your looks, and see compliance there.   140
Come raise the strain and grasp the full ton'd lyre:
The time, the theme, the place and all conspire.

Chaldean Woman

Air

See the ruddy morning smiling,
Hear the grove to bliss beguiling;
Zephyrs through the valley playing,
Streams along the meadow straying.

1st Priest

While these a constant revel keep,
Shall reason only bid me weep?
Hence, intruder! wee'l pursue
Nature, a better guide than you,   150

2nd Priest

Air

Every moment as it flows
Some peculiar pleasure owes:
Then let us, providently wise,
Sieze the Debtor as it flies.

Think not to morrow can repay
The pleasures that we lose to day;
To morrow's most unbounded store
Can but pay its proper score.

1st Priest

Recitative

But Hush, see, foremost of the Captive Choir,
The Master Prophet Grasps his full ton'd lyre.   160
Mark where he sits with executing art,
Feels for each tone, and speeds it to the heart.
See, inspiration fills his rising form,
Awful as clouds that nurse the growing storm,
And now his voice, accordant to the string,
Prepares our monarch's victories to sing.

1st Prophet

Air

From North, from South, from East, from West,
Conspiring foes shall come;
Tremble, thou vice polluted breast;
Blasphemers, all be dumb.   170

The tempest gathers all around,
On Babylon it lies;
Down with her, down, down to the ground,
She sinks, she groans, she dies.

2nd Prophet

Down with her, Lord, to lick the dust,
Ere yonder setting sun;
Serve her as she hath servd the just.
'Tis fixt, it shall be done.

1st Priest

Recitative

Enough! when slaves thus insolent presume,
The king himself shall judge and fix their doom.   180
Short-sighted wretches, have not you, and all
Beheld our power in Zedekiah's fall?

To yonder gloomy dungeon turn your eyes;
See where dethron'd your captive monarch lies.

Deprived of sight, and rankling in his chain,
He calls on death to terminate his pain.
Yet know ye slaves, that still remain behind
More Pondrous chains and dungeons more confind.

Chorus

Arise, all potent ruler, rise
And vindicate the peoples cause;   190
Till every tongue in every land
Shall offer up unfeign'd applause.

End of the 2nd Act

Act III

Scene as before

1st Priest

Recitative

Yes, my Companions, heaven's decrees are past,
And our fixt Empire shall for ever last;
In vain the madning prophet threatens woe,
In vain rebellion aims her secret blow;
Still shall our fame and growing power be spread,
And still our vengeance crush the guilty head.

Air

Coeval with man
Our Empire Began,   200
And never shall fall
Till ruin shakes all;
With the ruin of all
Shall Babylon fall.

2nd Prophet

Recitative

Tis thus that pride triumphant rears the head:
A little while and all her power is fled.
But ha! what means yon sadly plaintive train,
That this way slowly bends along the plain?
And now, methinks, a pallid coarse they bear
To yonder bank, and rest the body there.   210
Alas, too well mine eyes observant trace
The last remains of Judah's royal race:
Our monarch falls and now our fears are ore:
The Wretched Zedekiah is no more.

Air

Ye wretches who, by fortune's hate,
In want and sorrow groan,
Come ponder his severer fate,
And learns to bless your own.

Ye sons, from fortune's lap supply'd,
A while the bliss suspend;   220
Like yours his life began in pride,
Like his your lives may end.

2nd Prophet

Behold his squalid coarse with sorrow worn,
His wretched limbs with pondrous fetters torn;
Those eyeless orbs that shock with ghastly glare,
Those ill becoming robes and matted hair.
And shall not heaven for this its terrors shew,
And deal its angry vengeance on the foe?
How long, how long, Almighty lord of all,
Shall wrath vindictive threaten ere it fall?   230

Israelitish Woman

Air

As panting flies the hunted hind,
Where brooks refreshing stray,

And rivers through the valley wind,
That stop the hunters' way:

Thus we, O Lord, alike distresst,
For streams of mercy Long;
Those streams which chear the sore opprest,
And overwhelm the strong.

1st Prophet

Recitative

But whence that shout? Good heavens! amazement all!
See yonder tower just nodding to the fall: 240
See where an army covers all the ground,
Saps the strong wall, and pours destruction round.
The ruin smokes, destruction pours along;
How low the great, how feeble are the strong!
The foe prevails, the lofty walls recline:
O God of hosts the victory is thine!

Chorus of Israelites

Down with her, Lord, to lick the dust;
Let vengeance be begun:
Serve her as she hath servd the just,
And let thy will be done.   250

1st Priest

All, All is lost. The Syrian army fails;
Cyrus, the conqueror of the world, prevails.
Save us, O Lord, to thee tho Late we pray,
And give repentance but an hour's delay.

2nd Priest

Air

Thrice happy, who, in happy hour,
To heaven their praise bestow,
And own his all consuming power,
Before they feel the blow.

1st Prophet

Recitative

Now, Now's our time. Ye wretches bold and blind,
Brave but to God, and Cowards to Mankind;   260
Too late you seek that power unsought before:
Your wealth, your pride, your empire are no more.

Air

O Lucifer, thou son of morn,
Alike of heaven and man the foe,
Heaven, men, and all
Now press thy fall,
And sink thee lowest of the low.

2nd Priest

O Babylon, how art thou fallen,
Thy fall more dreadful from delay!
Thy streets forelorn   270
To wilds shall turn,
Where toads shall pant and vultures prey.

1st Prophet

Recitative

Such be her fate. But listen, from afar
The Clarion's note proclaims the finish'd war!
Cyrus, our Great restorer, is at hand,
And this way leads his formidable band.
Now give your songs of Sion to the wind,
And hail the benefactor of mankind:
He comes pursuant to divine decree,
To Chain the strong and set the captive free.   280

Chorus of Youths

Rise to raptures past expressing,
Sweeter from remember'd woes;

Cyrus comes, our wrongs redressing,
Comes to give the world repose.

Chorus of Virgins

Cyrus Comes, the world redressing,
Love and pleasure in his train,
Comes to heighten every blessing,
Comes to soften every pain.

Chorus of Youths and Virgins

Hail to him with mercy reigning,
Skilld in every peaceful art,   290
   Who from bonds our limbs unchaining,
   Only binds the willing heart.

Last Chorus

But Chief to thee, our God, our father, friend,
Let praise be given to all eternity;
O thou, without beginning, without end,
Let us, and all, begin, and end in thee!

Finis

The Traveller, or
A Prospect of Society

to the Rev. Henry Goldsmith

Dear Sir,
I am sensible that the friendship between us can acquire no
new force from the ceremonies of a Dedication; and perhaps it
demands an excuse thus to prefix your name to my attempts,
which you decline giving with your own. But as a part of this

Poem was formerly written to you from Switzerland, the whole can now, with propriety, be only inscribed to you. It will also throw a light upon many parts of it, when the reader understands that it is addressed to a man, who, despising Fame and Fortune, has retired early to Happiness and Obscurity, with an income of forty pounds a year.

I now perceive, my dear brother, the wisdom of your humble choice. You have entered upon a sacred office, where the harvest is great, and the labourers are but few; while you have left the field of Ambition, where the labourers are many, and the harvest not worth carrying away. But of all kinds of ambition, what from the refinement of the times, from differing systems of criticism, and from the divisions of party, that which pursues poetical fame, is the wildest.

Poetry makes a principal amusement among unpolished nations; but in a country verging to the extremes of refinement, Painting and Music come in for a share. As these offer the feeble mind a less laborious entertainment, they at first rival Poetry, and at length supplant her; they engross all that favour once shewn to her, and though but younger sisters, seize upon the elder's birth-right.

Yet, however this art may be neglected by the powerful, it is still in greater danger from the mistaken efforts of the learned to improve it. What criticism have we not heard of late in favour of blank verse, and Pindaric odes, choruses, anapests and iambics, alliterative care, and happy negligence. Every absurdity has now a champion to defend it, and as he is generally much in the wrong, so he has always much to say; for error is ever talkative.

But there is an enemy to this art still more dangerous, I mean party. Party entirely distorts the judgement, and destroys the taste. When the mind is once infected with this disease, it can only find pleasure in what contributes to encrease the distemper. Like the tyger, that seldom desists from pursuing man after having once preyed upon human flesh, the reader, who has once gratified his appetite with calumny, makes, ever after, the most agreeable feast upon murdered reputation. Such readers generally admire some half-witted thing, who wants to be thought a bold man, having lost the character of a wise one. Him they dignify with the name of poet; his tawdry lampoons are called satires, his turbulence is said to be force, and his phrenzy fire.

What reception a Poem may find, which has neither abuse, party, nor blank verse to support it, I cannot tell, nor am I solicitous to know. My aims are right. Without espousing the   50
cause of any party, I have attempted to moderate the rage of all. I have endeavoured to shew, that there may be equal happiness in states, that are differently governed from our own; that every state has a particular principle of happiness, and that this principle in each may be carried to a mischievous excess. There are few can judge, better than yourself, How far these positions are illustrated in this Poem.

 I am, dear Sir,

  Your most affectionate Brother,

        OLIVER GOLDSMITH

Remote, unfriended, melancholy, slow,
Or by the lazy Scheld, or wandering Po;
Or onward, where the rude Carinthian boor
Against the houseless stranger shuts the door;
Or where Campania's plain forsaken lies,
A weary waste expanding to the skies:
Where'er I roam, whatever realms to see,
My heart untravell'd fondly turns to thee;
Still to my brother turns, with ceaseless pain,
And drags at each remove a lengthening chain.   10

 Eternal blessings crown my earliest friend,
And round his dwelling guardian saints attend;
Blest be that spot, where chearful guests retire
To pause from toil, and trim their evening fire;
Blest that abode, where want and pain repair,
And every stranger finds a ready chair;
Blest be those feasts with simple plenty crown'd,
Where all the ruddy family around
Laugh at the jests or pranks that never fail,
Or sigh with pity at some mournful tale,   20
Or press the bashful stranger to his food,
And learn the luxury of doing good.

But me, not destin'd such delights to share,
My prime of life in wand'ring spent and care:
Impell'd, with steps unceasing, to pursue
Some fleeting good, that mocks me with the view;
That, like the circle bounding earth and skies,
Allures from far, yet, as I follow, flies;
My fortune leads to traverse realms alone,
And find no spot of all the world my own.   30

Even now, where Alpine solitudes ascend,
I sit me down a pensive hour to spend;
And, plac'd on high above the storm's career,
Look downward where an hundred realms appear;
Lakes, forests, cities, plains extending wide,
The pomp of kings, the shepherd's humbler pride.

When thus Creation's charms around combine,
Amidst the store, should thankless pride repine?
Say, should the philosophic mind disdain
That good, which makes each humbler bosom vain?   40
Let school-taught pride dissemble all it can,
These little things are great to little man;
And wiser he, whose sympathetic mind
Exults in all the good of all mankind.
Ye glittering towns, with wealth and splendour crown'd,
Ye fields, where summer spreads profusion round,
Ye lakes, whose vessels catch the busy gale,
Ye bending swains, that dress the flow'ry vale,
For me your tributary stores combine;
Creation's heir, the world, the world is mine.   50

As some lone miser visiting his store,
Bends at his treasure, counts, recounts it o'er;
Hoards after hoards his rising raptures fill,
Yet still he sighs, for hoards are wanting still:
Thus to my breast alternative passions rise,
Pleas'd with each good that heaven to man supplies:
Yet oft a sigh prevails, and sorrows fall,
To see the hoard of human bliss so small;
And oft I wish, amidst the scene, to find

Some sport to real happiness consign'd,   60
Where my worn soul, each wand'ring hope at rest,
May gather bliss to see my fellows blest.

  But where to find that happiest spot below,
Who can direct, when all pretend to know?
The shudd'ring tenant of the frigid zone
Boldly proclaims that happiest spot his own,
Extols the treasures of his stormy seas,
And his long nights of revelry and ease;
The naked Negro, panting at the line,
Boasts of his golden sands and palmy wine,   70
Basks in the glare, or stems the tepid wave,
And thanks his Gods for all the good they gave.
Such is the patriot's boast, where'er we roam,
His first best country ever is at home.

  And yet, perhaps, if countries we compare,
And estimate the blessings which they share;
Though patriots flatter, still shall wisdom find
An equal portion dealt to all mankind,
As different good, by Art or Nature given,
To different nations makes their blessings even.   80

  Nature, a mother kind alike to all,
Still grants her bliss at Labour's earnest call;
With food as well the peasant is supply'd
On Idra's cliffs as Arno's shelvy side;
And though the rocky crested summits frown,
These rocks, by custom, turn to beds of down.
From Art more various are the blessings sent;
Wealth, commerce, honor, liberty, content:
Yet these each other's power so strong contest,
That either seems destructive of the rest.   90
Where wealth and freedom reign contentment fails,
And honour sinks where commerce long prevails.
Hence every state, to one lov'd blessing prone,
Conforms and models life to that alone.
Each to the favourite happiness attends,
And spurns the plan that aims at other ends;

'Till, carried to excess in each domain,
This favourite good begets peculiar pain.

But let us try these truths with closer eyes,
And trace them through the prospect as it lies: 100
Here for a whole my proper cares resign'd,
Here let me sit in sorrow for mankind,
Like yon neglected shrub, at random cast,
That shades the steep, and sighs at every blast.

Far to the right, where Appennine ascends,
Bright as the summer, Italy extends;
Its uplands sloping deck the mountain's side,
Woods over woods, in gay theatric pride;
While oft some temple's mould'ring top between,
With venerable grandeur marks the scene.   110

Could Nature's bounty satisfy the breast,
The sons of Italy were surely blest.
Whatever fruits in different climes are found,
That proudly rise or humbly court the ground,
Whatever blooms in torrid tracts appear,
Whose bright succession decks the varied year;
Whatever sweets salute the northern sky
With vernal lives that blossom but to die;
These here disporting, own the kindred soil,
Nor ask luxuriance from the planter's toil;   120
While sea-born gales their gelid wings expand
To winnow fragrance round the smiling land.

But small the bliss that sense alone bestows,
And sensual bliss is all the nation knows.
In florid beauty groves and fields appear,
Man seems the only growth that dwindles here.
Contrasted faults through all his manners reign,
Though poor, luxurious, though submissive, vain,
Though grave, yet trifling, zealous, yet untrue,
And even in penance planning sins anew.   130
All evils here contaminate the mind,
That opulence departed leaves behind;

For wealth was theirs, nor far remov'd the date,
When commerce proudly flourish'd through the state:
At her command the palace learnt to rise,
Again the long-fall'n column sought the skies;
The canvas glow'd beyond even Nature warm,
The pregnant quarry teem'd with human form.
Till, more unsteady than the southern gale,
Commerce on other shores display'd her sail;   140
While nought remain'd of all that riches gave,
But towns unman'd, and lords without a slave:
And late the nation found, with fruitless skill,
Its former strength was but plethoric ill.

    Yet, still the loss of wealth is here supplied
By arts, the splendid wrecks of former pride;
From these the feeble heart and long fall'n mind
An easy compensation seem to find.
Here may be seen, in bloodless pomp array'd,
The paste-board triumph and the cavalcade;   150
Processions form'd for piety and love,
A mistress or a saint in every grove.
By sports like these are all their cares beguil'd,
The sports of children satisfy the child;
Each nobler aim represt by long controul,
Now sinks at last, or feebly mans the soul;
While low delights, succeeding fast behind,
In happier meanness occupy the mind:
As in those domes, where Caesars once bore sway,
Defac'd by time and tottering in decay,   160
There in the ruin, heedless of the dead,
The shelter-seeking peasant builds his shed,
And, wond'ring man could want the larger pile,
Exults, and owns his cottage with a smile.

    My soul turn from them, turn we to survey
Where rougher climes a nobler race display,
Where the bleak Swiss their stormy mansions tread,
And force a churlish soil for scanty bread;
No product here the barren hills afford,
But man and steel, the soldier and his sword.   170

No vernal blooms their torpid rocks array,
But winter lingering chills the lap of May;
No Zephyr fondly sues the mountain's breast,
But meteors glare and stormy glooms invest.
Yet still, even here, content can spread a charm,
Redress the clime, and all its rage disarm.
Though poor the peasant's hut, his feasts though small,
He sees his little lot, the lot of all;
Sees no contiguous palace rear its head
To shame the meanness of his humble shed;   180
No costly lord the sumptuous banquet deal
To make loath his vegetable meal;
But calm, and bred in ignorance and toil,
Each wish contracting, fits him to the soil.

Chearful at morn he wakes from short repose,
Breasts the keen air, and carrols as he goes;
With patient angle trolls the finny deep,
Or drives his vent'rous plow-share to the steep;
Or seeks the den where snow tracks mark the way,
And drags the struggling savage into day.   190
At night returning, every labour sped,
He sits him down the monarch of a shed;
Smiles by his chearful fire, and round surveys
His children looks, that brighten at the blaze:
While his lov'd partner, boastful of her hoard,
Displays her cleanly platter on the board;
And haply too some pilgrim, thither led,
With many a tale repays the nightly bed.

   Thus every good his native wilds impart,
Imprints the patriot passion on his heart,   200
And even those ills, that round his mansion rise,
Enhance the bliss his scanty fund supplies.
Dear is that shed to which his soul conforms,
And dear that hill which lifts him to the storms;
And as a child, when scaring sounds molest,
Clings close and closer to the mother's breast;
So the loud torrent, and the whirlwind's roar,
But bind him to his native mountains more.

Such are the charms to barren states assign'd;
Their wants but few, their wishes all confin'd.   210
Yet let them only share the praises due,
If few their wants, their pleasures are but few;
For every want, that stimulates the breast,
Become a source of pleasure when redrest.
Whence from such lands each pleasing science flies,
That first excites desire, and then supplies;
Unknown to them, when sensual pleasures cloy,
To fill the languid pause with finer joy;
Unknown those powers that raise the soul to flame,
Catch every nerve, and vibrate through the frame.   220
Their level life is but a smould'ring fire,
Unquench'd by want, unfann'd by strong desire;
Unfit for raptures, or, if raptures cheer
On some high festival of once a year,
In wild excess the vulgar breast takes fire,
Till, buried in debauch, the bliss expire.

   But not their joys alone thus coarsely flow:
Their morals, like their pleasures, are but low.
For, as refinement stops, from sire to son
Unalter'd, unimprov'd their manners run,   230
And love's and friendship's finely pointed dart
Fall blunted from each indurated heart.
Some sterner virtues o'er the mountain's breast
May sit, like falcons cow'ring on the nest;
But all the gentler morals, such as play
Through life's more cultur'd walks, and charm the way,
These far dispers'd, on timorous pinions fly,
To sport and flutter in a kinder sky.

   To kinder skies, where gentler manners reign,
I turn; and France displays her bright domain.   240
Gay sprightly land of mirth and social ease,
Pleas'd with thyself, whom all the world can please,
How often have I led thy sportive choir,
With tuneless pipe, beside the murmuring Loire?
Where shading elms along the margin grew,
And freshen'd from the wave the Zephyr flew;

And haply, tho' my harsh touch faltering still,
But mock'd all tune, and marr'd the dancer's skill;
Yet would the village praise my wond'rous power,
And dance, forgetful of the noon-tide hour.   250
Alike all ages. Dames of ancient days
Have led their children through the mirthful maze,
And the gay grandsire, skill'd in gestic lore,
Has frisk'd beneath the burthen of threescore.

So blest a life these thoughtless realms display,
Thus idly busy rolls their world away:
Theirs are those arts that mind to mind endear,
For honour forms the social temper here.
Honour, that praise which real merit gains,
Or even imaginary worth obtains,   260
Here passes current; paid from hand to hand,
It shifts in splendid traffic round the land:
From courts, to camps, to cottages it strays,
And all are taught an avarice of praise;
They please, are pleas'd, they give to get esteem,
Till, seeming blest, they grow to what they seem.

But while this softer art their bliss supplies,
It gives their follies also room to rise;
For praise too dearly lov'd, or warmly sought,
Enfeebles all internal strength of thought,   270
And the weak soul, within itself unblest,
Leans for all pleasure on another's breast.
Hence ostentation here, with tawdry art,
Pants for the vulgar praise which fools impart;
Here vanity assumes her pert grimace,
And trims her robes of frize with copper lace,
Here beggar pride defrauds her daily cheer,
To boast one splendid banquet once a year;
The mind still turns where shifting fashion draws,
Nor weighs the solid worth of self applause.   280

To men of other minds my fancy flies,
Embosom'd in the deep where Holland lies,
Methinks her patient sons before me stand,

Where the broad ocean leans against the land,
And, sedulous to stop the coming tide,
Lift the tall rampire's artificial pride.
Onward methinks, and diligently slow
The firm connected bulwark seems to grow;
Spreads its long arms amidst the watry roar,
Scoops out an empire, and usurps the shore.   290
While the pent ocean rising o'er the pile,
Sees an amphibious world beneath him smile;
The slow canal, the yellow blossom'd vale,
The willow tufted bank, the gliding sail,
The crowded mart, the cultivated plain,
A new creation rescu'd from his reign.

   Thus, while around, the wave-subjected soil
Impels the native to repeated toil,
Industrious habits in each bosom reign,
And industry begets a love of gain.   300
Hence all the good from opulence that springs,
With all those ills superfluous treasure brings,
Are here display'd. Their much-lov'd wealth imparts
Convenience, plenty, elegance, and arts;
But view them closer, craft and fraud appear,
Even liberty itself is barter'd here.
At gold's superior charms all freedom flies,
The needy sell it, and the rich man buys:
A land of tyrants, and a den of slaves,
Here wretches seek dishonourable graves,   310
And calmly bent, to servitude conform,
Dull as their lakes that slumber in the storm.

   Heavens! how unlike their Belgic fires of old!
Rough, poor, content, ungovernably bold;
War in each breast, and freedom on each brow;
How much unlike the sons of Britain now!

   Fir'd at the sound, my genius spreads her wing,
And flies where Britain courts the western spring;
Where lawns extend that scorn Arcadian pride,
And brighter streams than fam'd Hydaspis glide.   320

There all around the gentlest breezes stray,
There gentle music melts on every spray;
Creation's mildest charms are there combin'd,
Extremes are only in the master's mind;
Stern o'er each bosom reason holds her state.
With daring aims, irregularly great,
Pride in their port, defiance in their eye,
I see the lords of human kind pass by,
Intent on high designs, a thoughtful band,
By forms unfashion'd, fresh from Nature's hand;   330
Fierce in their native hardiness of soul,
True to imagin'd right, above controul,
While even the peasant boasts these rights to scan,
And learns to venerate himself as man.

Thine, Freedom, thine the blessings pictur'd here,
Thine are those charms that dazzle and endear;
Too blest indeed, were such without alloy,
But foster'd even by Freedom ills annoy:
That independence Britons prize too high,
Keeps man from man, and breaks the social tie;   340
The self-dependent lordlings stand alone,
All claims that bind and sweeten life unknown;
Here by the bonds of nature feebly held,
Minds combat minds, repelling and repell'd;
Ferments arise, imprison'd factions roar,
Represt ambition struggles round her shore,
Till over-wrought, the general system feels
Its motions stopt, or phrenzy fire the wheels.

Nor this the worst. As nature's ties decay,
As duty, love, and honour fail to sway,   350
Fictitious bonds, the bonds of wealth and law,
Still gather strength, and force unwilling awe.
Hence all obedience bows to these alone,
And talent sinks, and merit weeps unknown;
Till Time come, when, stript of all her charms,
The land of scholars, and the nurse of arms;
Where noble stems transmit the patriot flame,
Where kings have toil'd, and poets wrote for fame;

One sink of level avarice shall lie,
And scholars, soldiers, kings unhonor'd die.   360

    Yet think not, thus when Freedom's ills I state,
I mean to flatter kings, or court the great;
Ye powers of truth that bid my soul aspire,
Far from my bosom drive the low desire;
And thou fair freedom, taught alike to feel
The rabble's rage, and tyrant's angry streel;
Thou transitory flower, alike undone
By proud contempt, or favour's fostering sun,
Still may thy blooms the changeful clime endure,
I only would repress them to secure;   370
For just experience tells in every soil,
That those who think must govern those that toil,
And all that freedom's highest aims can reach,
Is but to lay proportion'd loads on each.
Hence, should one order disproportion'd grow,
Its double weight must ruin all below.
O then how blind to all that truth requires,
Who think it freedom when a part aspires!

Calm is my soul, nor apt to rise in arms,
Except when fast approaching danger warms: 380
But when contending chiefs blockade the throne,
Contracting regal power to stretch their own,
When I behold a factious band agree
To call it freedom, when themselves are free;
Each wanton judge new penal statutes draw,
Laws grind the poor, and rich men rule the law;
The wealth of climes, where savage nations roam,
Pillag'd from slaves, to purchase slaves at home;
Fear, pity, justice, indignation start,
Tear off reserve, and bare my swelling heart;   390
'Till half a patriot, half a coward grown,
I fly from petty tyrants to the throne.

    Yes, brother, curse with me that baleful hour,
When first ambition struck at regal power;
And thus, polluting honour in its source,

Gave wealth to sway the mind with double force.
Have we not seen, round Britain's peopled shore,
Her useful sons exchang'd for useful ore?
Seen all her triumphs but destruction haste,
Like flaring tapers brightening as they waste;   400
Seen opulence, her grandeur to maintain,
Lead stern depopulation in her train,
And over fields, where scatter'd hamlets rose,
In barren solitary pomp repose?
Have we not seen, at pleasure's lordly call,
The smiling long-frequented village fall;
Beheld the duteous son, the sire decay'd,
The modest matron, and the blushing maid,
Forc'd from their homes, a melancholy train,
To traverse climes beyond the western main;   410
Where wild Oswego spreads her swamps around,
And Niagara stuns with thund'ring sound?

   Even now, perhaps, as there some pilgrim strays
Through tangled forests, and through dangerous ways;
Where beasts with man divided empire claim,
And the brown Indian marks with murderous aim;
There, while above the giddy tempest flies,
And all around distressful yells arise,
The pensive exile, bending with his woe,
To stop too fearful, and too faint to go,   420
Casts a long look where England's glories shine,
And bids his bosom sympathize with mine.

   Vain, very vain, my weary search to find
That bliss which only centers in the mind:
Why have I stray'd, from pleasure and repose,
To seek a good each government bestows?
In every government, though terrors reign,
Though tyrant kings, or tyrant laws restrain,
How small, of all that human hearts endure,
That part which laws or kings can cause or cure.   430
Still to ourselves in every place consign'd,
Our own felicity we make or find:
With secret course, which no loud storms annoy,

Glides the smooth current of domestic joy.
The lifted ax, the agonizing wheel,
Luke's iron crown, and Damien's bed of steel,
To men remote from power but rarely known,
Leave reason, faith and conscience all our own.

THE END

A New Simile.
In the Manner of Swift

Long had I sought in vain to find
A likeness for the scribbling kind;
The modern scribbling kind, who write,
In wit, and sense, and nature's spite:
'Till reading, I forget what day on,
A chapter out of Took's Pantheon;
I think I met with something there,
To suit my purpose to a hair;
But let us not proceed too furious,
First please to turn to God Mercurius;   10
You'll find him pictured at full length
In book the second, page the tenth:
The stress of all my proofs on him I lay,
And now proceed we to our simile.

    Imprimis, pray observe his hat
Wings upon either side – mark that.
Well! what is it from thence we gather?
Why these denote a brain of feather.
A brain of feather! very right,
With wit that's flighty, learning light;   20
Such as to modern bard's decreed:
A just comparison, – proceed.

In the next place, his feet peruse,
Wings grow again from both his shoes;
Design'd no doubt, their part to bear,
And waft his godship through the air;
And here my simile unites,
For in a modern poet's flights,
I'm sure it may be justly said,
His feet are useful as his head.   30

Lastly, vouchsafe t' observe his hand,
Fill'd with a snake incircled wand;
By classic authors, term'd caducis,
And highly fam'd for several uses.
To wit – most wond'rously endu'd,
No poppy water half so good;
For let folks only get a touch,
It's soporific virtue's such,
Tho' ne'er so much awake before,
That quickly they begin to snore.   40
Add too, what certain writers tell,
With this he drives men's souls to hell.

Now to apply, begin we then;
His wand's a modern author's pen;
The serpents round about it twin'd
Denote him of the reptile kind;
Denote the rage with which he writes,
His frothy slaver, venom'd bites;
An equal semblance still to keep,
Alike too, both conduce to sleep.   50
This diff'rence only, as the God,
Drove souls to Tart'rus with his rod;
With his goosequill the scribing elf,
Instead of others, damns himself.

And here my simile almost tript,
Yet grant a word by way of postscript,
Moreover, Merc'ry had a failing:
Well! what of that? out with it – stealing;

In which all modern bards agree,
Being each as great a thief as he: 60
But ev'n this deities' existence,
Shall lend my simile assistance.
Our modern bards! why what a pox
Are they but senseless stones and blocks?

Verses in Reply to an Invitation to Dinner at Dr Baker's

Your mandate I got,
You may all go to pot;
Had your senses been right,
You'd have sent before night;
As I hope to be saved,
I put off being shaved;
For I could not make bold,
While the matter was cold,
To meddle in suds,
Or to put on my duds;   10
So tell Horneck and Nesbitt,
And Baker and his bit,
And Kauffman beside,
And the Jessamy bride,
With the rest of the crew,
The Reynoldses two,
Little Comedy's face,
And the Captain in lace.
(By the bye you may tell him,
I have something to sell him;   20
Of use I insist,
When he comes to enlist.
Your worship's must know
That a few days ago,

An order went out,
For the foot guards so stout
To wear tails in high taste,
Twelve inches at least:
Now I've got him a scale
To measure each tail,   30
To lengthen a short tail,
And a long one to curtail.) –
   Yet how can I when vext,
Thus stray from my text?
Tell each other to rue
Your Devonshire crew,
For sending so late
To one of my state.
But 'tis Reynolds's way
From wisdom to stray,   40
And Angelica's whim
To be frolick like him,
But, alas! your good worships, how could they be wiser,
When both have been spoil'd in today's Advertiser?

OLIVER GOLDSMITH

Epitaph on Edward Purdon

Here lies poor NED PURDON, from misery freed,
Who long was a bookseller's hack;
He led such a damnable life in this world, –
I don't think, he'll ever come back.

Epilogue to *The Sister: A Comedy*

What! five long acts – and all to make us wiser!
Our authoress sure has wanted an adviser.
Had she consulted *me*, she should have made
Her moral play a speaking masquerade,
Warm'd up each bustling scene, and in her rage
Have emptied all the Green-room on the stage.
My life on't, this had kept her play from sinking,
Have pleas'd our eyes, and sav'd the pain of thinking.
Well, since she thus has shewn her want of skill,
What if I give a masquerade? I will.   10
But how! ay, there's the rub! (*pausing*) I've got my cue:
The world's a masquerade! the masquers, you, you, you.
                                   [*To Boxes, Pit, Gallery*
Lud! what a groupe the motley scene discloses!
False wits, false wives, false virgins, and false spouses:
Statesmen who bridles on; and, close beside 'em,
Patriots, in party colour'd suits, that ride 'em.
There Hebes, turn'd of fifty, try once more,
To raise a flame in Cupids of threescore.
These, in their turn, with appetites as keen,
Deserting fifty, fasten on fifteen.   20
Miss, not yet full fifteen, with fire uncommon,
Flings down her sampler, and takes up the woman:
The little urchin smiles, and spreads her lure,
And tries to kill ere she's got power to cure.
Thus 'tis with all – Their chief and constant care
Is to seem every thing – but what they are.
Yon broad, bold, angry, spark, I fix my eye on,
Who seems t' have robb'd his visor from the lion,
Who frowns, and talks, and swears, with round parade,
Looking, as who should say, *Damme! who's afraid!* [*mimicking* 30
Strip but his vizor off, and sure I am,
You'll find his lionship a very lamb.
Yon politician, famous in debate,
Perhaps to vulgar eyes bestrides the state;
Yet, when he deigns his real shape t'assume,
He turns old woman, and bestrides a broom.

Yon patriot too, who presses on your sight,
And seems to every gazer all in white;
If with a bribe his candour you attack,
He bows, turns round, and whip – the man's a black!   40
Yon critic too – but whither do I run?
If I proceed, our bard will be undone!
Well then, a truce, since she requests it too;
Do you spare her, and I'll for once spare you.

The Deserted Village

To Sir Joshua Reynolds

Dear Sir,
I can have no expectations in an address of this kind, either to
add to your reputation, or to establish my own. You can gain
nothing from my admiration, as I am ignorant of that art in
which you are said to excel; and I may lose much by the
severity of your judgment, as few have a juster taste in poetry
than you. Setting interest therefore aside, to which I never
paid much attention, I must be indulged at present in
following my affections. The only dedication I ever made was
to my brother, because I loved him better than most other   10
men. He is since dead. Permit me to inscribe this Poem to you.

   How far you may be pleased with the versification and
mere mechanical parts of this attempt, I don't pretend to
enquire; but I know you will object (and indeed several of our
best and wisest friends concur in the opinion) that the
depopulation it deplores is no where to be seen, and the
disorders it laments are only to be found in the poet's own
imagination. To this I can scarce make any other answer
than that I sincerely believe what I have written; that I have
taken all possible pains, in my country excursions, for these   20
four or five years past, to be certain of what I alledge, and that
all my views and enquiries have led me to believe those
miseries real, which I here attempt to display. But this is not

the place to enter into an enquiry, whether the country be depopulating, or not; the discussion would take up much room, and I should prove myself, at best, an indifferent politician, to tire the reader with a long preface, when I want his unfatigued attention to a long poem.

In regretting the depopulation of the country, I inveigh against the increase of our luxuries; and here also I expect the shout of modern politicians against me. For twenty or thirty years past, it has been the fashion to consider luxury as one of the greatest national advantages; and all the wisdom of antiquity in that particular, as erroneous. Still however, I must remain a professed ancient on that head, and continue to think those luxuries prejudicial to states, by which so many vices are introduced, and so many kingdoms have been undone. Indeed so much has been poured out of late on the other side of the question, that, merely for the sake of novelty and variety, one would sometimes wish to be in the right.

I am,
   Dear Sir,
      Your sincere friend,
        and ardent admirer,

                       OLIVER GOLDSMITH

Sweet Auburn, loveliest village of the plain,
Where health and plenty cheared the labouring swain,
Where smiling spring its earliest visit paid,
And parting summer's lingering blooms delayed,
Dear lovely bowers of innocence and ease,
Seats of my youth, when every sport could please,
How often have I loitered o'er thy green,
Where humble happiness endeared each scene;
How often have I paused on every charm,
The sheltered cot, the cultivated farm,
The never failing brook, the busy mill,
The decent church that topt the neighbouring hill,
The hawthorn bush, with seats beneath the shade,
For talking age and whispering lovers made.
How often have I blest the coming day,
When toil remitting lent its turn to play,

And all the village train from labour free
Led up their sports beneath the spreading tree,
While many a pastime circled in the shade,
The young contending as the old surveyed;   20
And many a gambol frolicked o'er the ground,
And slights of art and feats of strength went round.
And still as each repeated pleasure tired,
Succeeding sports the mirthful band inspired;
The dancing pair that simply sought renown
By holding out to tire each other down,
The swain mistrustless of his smutted face,
While secret laughter tittered round the place,
The bashful virgin's side-long looks of love,
The matron's glance that would those looks reprove.   30
These were thy charms, sweet village; sports like these,
With sweet succession, taught even toil to please;
These round thy bowers their chearful influence shed,
These were thy charms – But all these charms are fled.

   Sweet smiling village, loveliest of the lawn,
Thy sports are fled, and all thy charms withdrawn;
Amidst thy bowers the tyrant's hand is seen,
And desolation saddens all thy green:
One only master grasps the whole domain,
And half a tillage stints thy smiling plain;   40
No more thy glassy brook reflects the day,
But choaked with sedges, works its weedy way.
Along thy glades, a solitary guest,
The hollow sounding bittern guards its nest;
Amidst thy desert walks the lapwing flies,
And tires their echoes with unvaried cries.
Sunk are thy bowers in shapeless ruin all,
And the long grass o'ertops the mouldering wall,
And trembling, shrinking from the spoiler's hand,
Far, far away thy children leave the land.   50

   Ill fares the land, to hastening ills a prey,
Where wealth accumulates, and men decay;
Princes and lords may flourish, or may fade;
A breath can make them, as a breath has made.

But a bold peasantry, their country's pride,
When once destroyed, can never be supplied,

   A time there was, ere England's griefs began,
When every rood of ground maintained its man;
For him light labour spread her wholesome store,
Just gave what life required, but gave no more.   60
His best companions, innocence and health;
And his best riches, ignorance of wealth.

   But times are altered; trade's unfeeling train
Usurp the land and dispossess the swain;
Along the lawn, where scattered hamlets rose,
Unwieldy wealth, and cumbrous pomp repose;
And every want to oppulence allied,
And every pang that folly pays to pride.
These gentle hours that plenty bade to bloom,
Those calm desires that asked but little room,   70
Those healthful sports that graced the peaceful scene,
Lived in each look, and brightened all the green;
These far departing seek a kinder shore,
And rural mirth and manners are no more.

   Sweet Auburn! parent of the blissful hour,
Thy glades forlorn confess the tyrant's power.
Here as I take my solitary rounds,
Amidst thy tangling walks, and ruined grounds,
And, many a year elapsed, return to view
Where once the cottage stood, the hawthorn grew,   80
Remembrance wakes with all her busy train,
Swells at my breast, and turns the past to pain.

   In all my wanderings round this world of care,
In all my griefs – and GOD has given my share –
I still had hopes my latest hours to crown,
Amidst these humble bowers to lay me down;
To husband out life's taper at the close,
And keep the flame from wasting by respose.
I still had hopes, for pride attends us still,
Amidst the swains to shew my book-learned skill,   90

Around my fire an evening groupe to draw,
And tell of all I felt, and all I saw;
And, as an hare whom hounds and horns pursue,
Pants to the place from whence at first she flew,
I still had hopes, my long vexations past,
Here to return – and die at home at last.

O blest retirement, friend to life's decline,
Retreats from care that never must be mine,
How happy he who crowns in shades like these,
A youth of labour with an age of ease;   100
Who quits a world where strong temptations try,
And, since 'tis hard to combat, learns to fly.
For him no wretches, born to work and weep,
Explore the mine, or tempt the dangerous deep;
No surly porter stands in guilty state
To spurn imploring famine from the gate,
But on he moves to meet his latter end,
Angels around befriending virtue's friend;
Bends too the grave with unperceived decay,
While resignation gently slopes the way;   110
And all his prospects brightening to the last,
His Heaven commences ere the world be past!

Sweet was the sound when oft at evening's close,
Up yonder hill the village murmur rose;
There as I past with careless steps and slow,
The mingling notes came softened from below;
The swain responsive as the milk-maid sung,
The sober herd that lowed to meet their young;
The noisy geese that gabbled o'er the pool,
The playful children just let loose from school;   120
The watch-dog's voice that bayed the whispering wind,
And the loud laugh that spoke the vacant mind,
These all in sweet confusion sought the shade,
And filled each pause the nightingale had made.
But now the sounds of population fail,
No chearful murmurs fluctuate in the gale,
No busy steps the grass-grown foot-way tread,
For all the bloomy flush of life is fled.

All but yon widowed, solitary thing
That feebly bends beside the plashy spring;   130
She, wretched matron, forced, in age, for bread,
To strip the brook with mantling cresses spread,
To pick her wintry faggot from the thorn,
To seek her nightly shed, and weep till morn;
She only left of all the harmless train,
The sad historian of the pensive plain.

Near yonder copse, where once the garden smil'd,
And still where many a garden flower grows wild;
There, where a few torn shrubs the place disclose,
The village preacher's modest mansion rose.   140
A man he was, to all the country dear,
And passing rich with forty pounds a year;
Remote from towns he ran his godly race,
Nor ere had changed, nor wish'd to change his place;
Unpractised he to fawn, or seek for power,
By doctrines fashioned to the varying hour;
Far other aims his heart had learned to prize,
More skilled to raise the wretched than to rise.
His house was known to all the vagrant train,
He chid their wanderings, but relieved their pain;   150

The long remembered beggar was his guest,
Whose beard descending swept his aged breast;
The ruined spendthrift, now no longer proud,
Claimed kindred there, and had his claims allowed;
The broken soldier, kindly bade to stay,
Sate by his fire, and talked the night away;
Wept o'er his wounds, or tales of sorrow done,
Shouldered his crutch, and shewed how fields were won.
Pleased with his guests, the good man learned to glow,
And quite forgot their vices in their woe;   160
Careless their merits, or their faults to scan,
His pity gave ere charity began.

Thus to relieve the wretched was his pride,
And even his failings leaned to Virtue's side;
But in his duty prompt at every call,

He watched and wept, he prayed and felt, for all.
And, as a bird each fond endearment tries,
To tempt its new fledged offspring to the skies;
He tried each art, reproved each dull delay,
Allured to brighter worlds, and led the way.   170

Beside the bed where parting life was layed,
And sorrow, guilt, and pain, by turns dismayed,
The reverend champion stood. At his control,
Despair and anguish fled the struggling soul;
Comfort came down the trembling wretch to raise,
And his last faultering accents whispered praise.

At church, with meek and unaffected grace,
His looks adorned the venerable place;
Truth from his lips prevailed with double sway,
And fools, who came to scoff, remained to pray.   180
The service past, around the pious man,
With steady zeal each honest rustic ran;
Even children followed with endearing wile,
And plucked his gown, to share the good man's smile.
His ready smile a parent's warmth exprest,
Their welfare pleased him, and their cares distrest;
To them his heart, his love, his griefs were given,
But all his serious thoughts had rest in Heaven.
As some tall cliff that lifts its awful form,
Swells from the vale, and midway leaves the storm,   190
Tho' round its breast the rolling clouds are spread,
Eternal sunshine settles on its head.

Beside yon straggling fence that skirts the way,
With blossomed furze unprofitably gay,
There, in his noisy mansion, skill'd to rule,
The village master taught his little school;
A man severe he was, and stern to view,
I knew him well, and every truant knew;
Well had the boding tremblers learned to trace
The day's disasters in his morning face;   200
Full well they laugh'd with counterfeited glee,
At all his jokes, for many a joke had he;

Full well the busy whisper circling round,
Conveyed the dismal tidings when he frowned;
Yet he was kind, or if severe in aught,
The love he bore to learning was in fault;
The village all declared how much he knew;
'Twas certain he could write, and cypher too;
Lands he could measure, terms and tides presage,
And even the story ran that he could gauge.   210
In arguing too, the parson owned his skill,
For e'en tho' vanquished, he could argue still;
While words of learned length, and thundering sound,
Amazed the gazing rustics ranged around,
And still they gazed, and still the wonder grew,
That one small head could carry all he knew.

   But past is all his fame. The very spot
Where many a time he triumphed, is forgot.
Near yonder thorn, that lifts its head on high,
Where once the sign-post caught the passing eye,   220
Low lies that house where nut-brown draughts inspired,
Where grey-beard mirth and smiling toil retired,
Where village statesmen talked with looks profound,
And news much older than their ale went round.
Imagination fondly stoops to trace
The parlour splendours of that festive place;
The white-washed wall, the nicely sanded floor,
The vanished clock that clicked behind the door;
The chest contrived a double debt to pay,
A bed by night, a chest of drawers by day;   230
The pictures placed for ornament and use,
The twelve good rules, the royal game of goose;
The hearth, except when winter chill'd the day,
With aspen boughs, and flowers, and fennel gay,
While broken tea-cups, wisely kept for shew,
Ranged o'er the chimney, glistened in a row.

   Vain transitory splendours! Could not all
Reprieve the tottering mansion from its fall!
Obscure it sinks, nor shall it more impart
An hour's importance to the poor man's heart;   240

Thither no more the peasant shall repair
To sweet oblivion of his daily care;
No more the farmer's news, the barber's tale,
No more the wood-man's ballad shall prevail;
No more the smith his dusky brow shall clear,
Relax his ponderous strength, and lean to hear;
The host himself no longer shall be found
Careful to see the mantling bliss go round;
Nor the coy maid, half willing to be prest,
Shall kiss the cup to pass it to the rest.   250

    Yes! let the rich deride, the proud disdain;
These simple blessings of the lowly train,
To me more dear, congenial to my heart,
One native charm, than all the gloss of art;
Spontaneous joys, where Nature has its play,
The soul adopts, and owns their first born sway,
Lightly they frolic o'er the vacant mind,
Unenvied, unmolested, unconfined.
But the long pomp, the midnight masquerade,
With all the freaks of wanton wealth arrayed,   260
In these, ere triflers half their wish obtain,
The toiling pleasure sickens into pain;
And, even while fashion's brightest arts decoy,
The heart distrusting asks, if this be joy.

    Ye friends to truth, ye statesmen who survey
The rich man's joy's encrease, the poor's decay,
'Tis yours to judge, how wide the limits stand
Between a splendid and an happy land.
Proud swells the tide with loads of freighted ore,
And shouting Folly hails them from her shore;   270
Hoards, even beyond the miser's wish abound,
And rich men flock from all the world around.
Yet count our gains. This wealth is but a name
That leaves our useful products still the same.
Not so the loss. The man of wealth and pride,
Takes up a space that many poor supplied;
Space for this lake, his park's extended bounds,
Space for his horses, equipage, and hounds;

The robe that wraps his limbs in silken sloth,
Has robbed the neighbouring fields of half their growth;   280
His seat, where solitary sports are seen,
Indignant spurns the cottage from the green;
Around the world each needful product flies,
For all the luxuries the world supplies.
While thus the land adorned for pleasure all
In barren splendour feebly waits the fall.

    As some fair female unadorned and plain,
Secure to please while youth confirms her reign,
Slights every borrowed charm that dress supplies,
Nor shares with art the triumph of her eyes.   290
But when those charms are past, for charms are frail,
When time advances, and when lovers fail,
She then shines forth sollicitous to bless,
In all the glaring impotence of dress.
Thus fares the land, by luxury betrayed,
In nature's simplest charms at first arrayed,
But verging to decline, its splendours rise,
Its vistas strike, its palaces surprize;
While scourged by famine from the smiling land,
The mournful peasant leads his humble band;   300
And while he sinks without one arm to save,
The country blooms – a garden, and a grave.

    Where then, ah, where shall poverty reside,
To scape the pressure of contiguous pride?
If to some common's fenceless limits strayed,
He drives his flock to pick the scanty blade,
Those fenceless fields the sons of wealth divide,
And even the bare-worn common is denied.

    If to the city sped – What waits him there?
To see profusion that he must not share;   310
To see ten thousand baneful arts combined
To pamper luxury, and thin mankind;
To see those joys the sons of pleasure know,
Extorted from his fellow-creature's woe.
Here, while the courtier glitters in brocade,

There the pale artist plies the sickly trade;
Here, while the proud their long drawn pomps display,
There the black gibbet glooms beside the way.
The dome where pleasure holds her midnight reign,
Here richly deckt admits the gorgeous train, 320
Tumultuous grandeur crowds the blazing square,
The rattling chariots clash, the torches glare;
Sure scenes like these no troubles ere annoy!
Sure these denote one universal joy!
Are these thy serious thoughts? – Ah, turn thine eyes
Where the poor houseless shivering female lies.
She once, perhaps, in village plenty blest,
Has wept at tales of innocence distrest;
Her modest looks the cottage might adorn,
Sweet as the primrose peeps beneath the thorn; 330
Now lost to all; her friends, her virtue fled,
Near her betrayer's door she lays her head,
And pinch'd with cold, and shrinking from the shower,
With heavy heart deplores that luckless hour,
When idly first, ambitious of the town,
She left her wheel and robes of country brown.

Do thine, sweet Auburn, thin, the loveliest train,
Do thy fair tribes participate her pain?
Even now, perhaps, by cold and hunger led,
At proud men's doors they ask a little bread! 340

Ah, no. To distant climes, a dreary scene,
Where half the convex world intrudes between,
Through torrid tracts with fainting steps they go,
Where wild Altama murmurs to their woe.
Far different there from all that charm'd before,
The various terrors of that horrid shore.
Those blazing suns that dart a downward ray,
And fiercely shed intolerable day;
Those matted woods where birds forget to sing,
But silent bats in drowsy clusters cling, 350
Those poisonous fields with rank luxuriance crowned
Where the dark scorpion gathers death around;
Where at each step the stranger fears to wake

The rattling terrors of the vengeful snake;
Where crouching tigers wait their hapless prey,
And savage men more murderous still than they;
While oft in whirls the mad tornado flies,
Mingling the ravaged landscape with the skies.
Far different these from every former scene,
The cooling brook, the grassy vested green,   360
The breezy covert of the warbling grove,
That only sheltered thefts of harmless love.

    Good Heaven! what sorrows gloom'd that parting day,
That called them from their native walks away;
When the poor exiles, every pleasure past,
Hung round their bowers, and fondly looked their last,
And took a long farewell, and wished in vain
For seats like these beyond the western main;
And shuddering still to face the distant deep,
Returned and wept, and still returned to weep.   370
The good old sire, the first prepared to go
To new found worlds, and wept for others' woe.
But for himself, in conscious virtue brave,
He only wished for worlds beyond the grave.
His lovely daughter, lovelier in her tears,
The fond companions of his helpless years,
Silent went next, neglectful of her charms,
And left a lover's for a father's arms.
With louder plaints the mother spoke her woes,
And blest the cot where every pleasure rose;   380
And kist her thoughtless babes with many a tear,
And claspt them close in sorrow doubly dear;
Whilst her fond husband strove to lend relief
In all the silent manliness of grief.

    O luxury! Thou curst by heaven's decree,
How ill exchanged are things like these for thee!
How do thy potions with insidious joy,
Diffuse their pleasures only to destroy!
Kingdoms by thee, to sickly greatness grown,

Boast of a florid vigour not their own. 390
At every draught more large and large they grow,
A bloated mass of rank unwieldy woe;
Till sapped their strength, and every part unsound,
Down, down they sink, and spread a ruin round.

  Even now the devastation is begun,
And half the business of destruction done;
Even now, methinks, as pondering here I stand,
I see the rural virtues leave the land.
Down where yon anchoring vessel spreads the sail
That idly waiting flaps with every gale, 400
Downward they move, a melancholy band,
Pass from the shore, and darken all the strand.
Contented toil, and hospitable care,
And kind connubial tenderness, are there:
And piety with wishes placed above,
And steady loyalty, and faithful love.
And thou, sweet Poetry, thou loveliest maid,
Still first to fly where sensual joys invade;
Unfit in these degenerate times of shame,
To catch the heart, or strike for honest fame; 410
Dear charming nymph, neglected and decried,
My shame in crowds, my solitary pride.
Thou source of all my bliss, and all my woe,
That found'st me poor at first, and keep'st me so;
Thou guide by which the nobler arts excell,
Thou nurse of every virtue, fare thee well.
Farewell, and O where'er thy voice be tried,
On Torno's cliffs, or Pambamarca's side,
Whether where equinoctial fervours glow,
Or winter wraps the polar world in snow, 420
Still let thy voice prevailing over time,
Redress the rigours of the inclement clime;
Aid slighted truth, with thy persuasive strain
Teach erring man to spurn the rage of gain;
Teach him that states of native strength possest,
Tho' very poor may still be very blest;

That trade's proud empire hastes to swift decay,
As ocean sweeps the labour'd mole away;
While self dependent power can time defy,
As rocks resist the billows and the sky.   430

FINIS

Epitaph on Thomas Parnell

This tomb, inscrib'd to gentle Parnell's name,
May speak our gratitude, but not his fame.
What heart but feels his sweetly-moral lay,
That leads to Truth thro' Pleasure's flow'ry way?
Celestial themes confess'd his tuneful aid;
And Heav'n, that lent him Genius, was repaid.
Needless to him the tribute we bestow,
The transitory breath of Fame below:
More lasting rapture from his Works shall rise,
While Converts thank their Poet in the skies.

The Haunch of Venison.
A Poetical Epistle to Lord Clare

Thanks my Lord for your venison for finer or fatter
Never ranged in a forest or smoak'd on a platter
The haunch was a picture for painters to study
The fat was so white and the lean was so ruddy
Tho' my stomach was sharp I could scarce help regretting
To spoil such a delicate picture by eating
I had thought in my chamber to place it in view

To be shewn to my friends as a piece of virtu
As in some Irish houses where things are so so
One Gammon of Bacon hangs up for a shew   10
But for eating a rasher of what they take pride in
They'd as soon think of eating the pan it is fried in
But hold – Let us pause – Don't I hear you pronounce
This tale of the Bacon a damnable bounce
Well suppose it a bounce, sure a poet may try
By a bounce now and then to get courage to fly
But my Lord its no bounce I protest in my turn
It's a truth, and your Lordship may ask Mr. Burn.
To go on with my tale as I gaz'd on the haunch
I thought of a friend that was trusty and staunch   20
So I cut it and sent it to Reynolds undrest
To paint it, or eat it, just as he liked best.
Of the neck and the breast I had next to dispose
'Twas a neck and a breast that might rival Monroe's
But in parting with these I was puzled again
With the how, and the who, and the where and the when
There's Howard and Coley and Haworth and Hiff
I think they love venison – I know they love beef
There's my country man Higgins Oh let him alone
For making a blunder or picking a bone   30
But hang it, to poets who seldom can eat
Your very good mutton's a very good treat
Such Dainties to them, their health It might hurt
Its like sending them ruffles when wanting a shirt
     While thus I debated in reverie centered
An acquaintance, a friend as he called himself entered
An under bred fine spoken fellow was he
And he smiled as he look'd at the venison and me
     What have we got here Ay this is good eating
Your own I suppose. Or is it in waiting.   40
     Why whose should it be cried I with a flounce
I get these things often, but that was a bounce.
Some Lords my acquaintance that settle the nation
Are pleas'd to be kind – but I hate ostentation.
     If that be the case then cried he very gay
I'm glad I have taken this house in my way
Tomorrow you take a poor dinner with me

No words I insist on't precisely at three.
We'll have Johnson and Burke, all the wits will be there
My acquaintance is slight or I'd ask my Lord Clare   50
And now that I think on't, as I am a sinner
We wanted this venison to make out the dinner
What say you, a pasty – It shall, and it must
And my wife little Kisty is famous for crust.
Here porter this venison with me to mile end
No stirring I beg my dear friend, my dear friend.
Thus snatching his hat he brush'd off like the wind
And the porter and eatables followed behind.

    Left alone to reflect having emptied my shelf
And nobody with me at Sea but myself.   60
Tho' I could not help thinking my gentle man hasty
Yet Johnson and Burke and a good venison pasty
Were things that I never disliked in my life
Tho' clogged with a coxcomb and Kisty his wife
So next day in due splendour to make my approach
I drove to his door in my own Hackney Coach.

    When come to the place where we all were to dine
A chair lumbered closet, just twelve feet by nine
My friend bid me welcome, but struck me quite dumb
With tidings that Johnson and Burke could not come   70
For I knew it he cried, both eternally fail
The one with his speeches the other with Thrale
But no matter I'll warrant we'll make up the party
With two full as clever and ten times as hearty
The one is a Scotchman and other a jew
They both of them merry and authors like you
The one writes the snarler, the other the scourge
Some think he writes Cinna, he owns to Panurge
While thus he describ'd them by trade and by name
They entered and dinner was served as they came   80

    At the top a fried liver and bacon was seen
At the bottom was tripe in a swinging Tureen
At the sides there was spinnage and pudding made hot
In the middle a place where the pasty was not.
Now My Lord as for tripe its my utter aversion
And your bacon I hate like a Turk or a Persian
So there I sate stuck like a horse in a pound

While the bacon and liver went merrily round.
But what vex't me most was that dam'd Scottish rogue
With his long winded speeches and smiles and his brogue   90
And Madam quoth he may this bit be my poison
A prettier dinner I never set eyes on
Pray a slice of your liver, tho may I be curst
But I've eat of your tripe till I'm ready to burst
The tripe quoth the Jew with his chocolate cheek
I could dine on this tripe seven days in the week
I like these here dinners so pretty and small
But your friend there the Doctor eats nothing at all
O ho quoth my friend he'll come on in a trice
He's keeping a corner for something that's nice!   100
There's a pasty – A pasty repeated the Jew
I don't care if I keep a corner for't too:
What the Deil Mon a pasty reechoed the Scot
Tho' splitting I'd still keep a corner for that.
We'll all keep a corner the lady cried out
We'll all keep a corner was echoed about
While thus we resolved and the pasty delay'd
With looks quite petrified entered the maid
A visage so sad and so pale with affright
Waked Priam by drawing his curtains by night   110
But we quickly found out for who could mistake her
That she came with some terrible news from the baker
And so it fell out for that negligent sloven
Had shut out the pasty on shutting his oven.
Sad Philomel thus – but let similes drop
And now that I think on't the story may stop
To be plain my good Lord its but labour misplact
To send such good verses to one of your taste
You've got an odd something, a kind of discerning
A relish, a taste sickened over by learning   120
At least it's your temper, it's very well known
That you think very slightly of all that's your own
So perhaps in your habits of thinking amiss
You may make a mistake and think slightly of this.

Prologue to *Zobeide*

In these bold times, when Learning's sons explore
The distant climate and the savage shore;
When wise *Astronomers* to *India* steer,
And quit for *Venus*, many a brighter here;
When *Botanists*, all cold to smiles and dimpling,
Forsake the fair, and patiently – go simpling;
While every bosom swells with wond'rous scenes,
Priests, cannibals, and hoity-toity queens:
Our bard into the general spirit enters,
And fits his little frigate for adventures: 10
With *Scythian stores*, and trinkets deeply laden,
He this way steers his course in hopes of trading –
Yet ere he lands he's ordered me before,
To make an observation on the shore.
Where are we driven? Our reck'ning sure is lost!
This seems a barren and a dangerous coast.
Lord what a sultry climate am I under!
Yon ill-foreboding cloud seems big with thunder.
                            (*to the Upper Gallery*)
There Mangroves spread, and larger than I've seen 'em –
                            (*to the Pit*)
Here trees of stately size – and monkies in 'em –   20
                        (*to the pidgeon holes*)
Here ill-condition'd oranges abound –   (*to the Stage*)
And apples (*taking up and tasting*) *bitter* apples strew the ground.
The place is uninhabited I fear;
I heard a hissing – there are serpents here!
O there the natives are – a savage race!
The men have tails, the women paint the face!
No doubt they're all barbarians – Yes, 'tis so,
I'll try to make palaver with them though;   (*makes signs*)
'Tis best however keeping at a distance.
Good Savages, our Captain craves assistance;   30
Our ship's well stor'd; – in yonder creek we've laid her,
His honour is no mercenary trader;
To make you finer is his sole endeavour;

He seeks no benefit, content with favour.
This is his first adventure, lend him aid,
Or you may chance to spoil a thriving trade.
His goods he hopes are prime, and brought from far,
Equally fit for gallantry and war.
What no reply to promises so ample?
I'd best step back – and order up a sample.   40

Threnodia Augustalis

Overture a solemn Dirge

AIR. TRIO

Arise ye sons of worth, arise
And waken every note of woe,
When truth and virtue reach the skies,
'Tis ours to weep the want below.

CHORUS

When truth and virtue reach the skies,
'Tis ours to weep the want below.

MAN SPEAKER

The praise attending pomp and power,
The incense given to kings,
Are but the trappings of an hour,
Mere transitory things!   10
The base bestow them; but the good agree
To spurn the venal gifts as flattery. —
But when to pomp, and power, are join'd
An equal dignity of mind;
When titles are the smallest claim;
When wealth, and rank, and noble blood,

But aid the power of doing good,
Then all their trophies last – and flattery turns to fame!

  Blest spirit thou, whose fame just born to bloom,
Shall spread and flourish from the tomb,   20
How hast thou left mankind for heaven!
Even now reproach and faction mourn,
And, wondering how their rage was born,
Request to be forgiven!
Alas! they never had thy hate;
Unmoved in conscious rectitude
Thy towering mind self-centered stood,
Nor wanted Man's opinion to be great.
In vain, to charm thy ravished sight,
A thousand gifts would fortune send;   30
In vain, to drive thee from the right,
A thousand sorrows urged thy end:
Like some well-fashion'd arch thy patience stood,
And purchased strength from its encreasing load.
Pain met thee like a friend that set thee free,
Affliction still is virtue's opportunity!
Virtue, on herself relying,
Every passion hush'd to rest,
Loses every pain of dying
In the hopes of being blest.   40
Every added pang she suffers,
Some increasing good bestows,
And every shock that malice offers,
Only rocks her to repose.

SONG, BY A MAN. *Affettuoso*

Virtue, on herself relying,
Every passion hush'd to rest,
Loses every pain of dying
In the hopes of being blest.
Every added Pang she suffers,
Some encreasing good bestows,   50

Every shock that malice offers,
Only rocks her to repose.

WOMAN SPEAKER

Yet ah! what terrors frown'd upon her fate,
Death with its formidable band,
Fever, and pain, and a pale consumptive care,
Determined took their stand.
Nor did the cruel ravagers design
To finish all their efforts at a blow;
But, mischievously slow,
They robbed the relic and defac'd the shrine. —   60
With unavailing grief,
Despairing of relief,
Her weeping children round,
Beheld each hour
Death's growing pow'r,
And trembled as he frown'd.
As helpless friends who view from shore
The labouring ship, and hear the tempest roar,
While winds and waves their wishes cross;
They stood while hope and comfort fail   70
Not to assist, but to bewail
The inevitable loss. —
Relentless tyrant, at thy call
How do the good, the virtuous fall?
Truth, beauty, worth, and all that most engage,
But wake thy vengeance and provoke thy rage.

When vice my dart and scythe supply,
How great a king of Terrors I!
If folly, fraud, your hearts engage,
Tremble ye mortals at my rage.   80

Fall, round me fall ye little things,
Ye statesmen, warriors, poets, kings,
If virtue fail her counsel sage
Tremble ye mortals at my rage.

MAN SPEAKER

Yet let that wisdom, urged by her example,
Teach us to estimate what all must suffer:
Let us prize death as the best gift of nature,
As a safe inn where weary travellers,
When they have journyed thro' a world of cares,
May put off life and be at rest for ever.   90
Groans, weeping friends, indeed, and gloomy sables
May oft distract us with their sad solemnity.
The preparation is the executioner.
Death, when unmasked, shews me a friendly face,
And is a terror only at a distance:
For as the line of life conducts me on
To death's great court, the prospect seems more fair;
'Tis nature's kind retreat, that's always open
To take us in when we have drain'd the cup
Of life, or worn our days to wretchedness. —   100
In that secure, serene retreat,
Where all the humble, all the great,
Promiscuously recline;
Where wildly huddled to the eye,
The beggar's pouch and prince's purple lie,
May every bliss be thine.
And ah! blest spirit, wheresoe'er thy flight,
Through rolling worlds, or fields of liquid light,
May cherubs welcome their expected guest,
May saints with songs receive thee to their rest,   110
May peace that claim'd while here thy warmest love,
May blissful endless peace be thine above.

SONG, BY A WOMAN. *Amoroso*

Lovely lasting peace below,
Comforter of every woe,
Heavenly born, and bred on high,
To crown the favourites of the sky:
Lovely lasting peace appear,
This world itself, if thou art here,
Is once again with Eden blest,
And man contains it in his breast.   120

WOMAN SPEAKER

Our vows are heard! Long, long to mortal eyes,
Her soul was fitting to its kindred skies:
Celestial-like her bounty fell,
Where modest want and patient sorrow dwell.
Want pass'd for merit at her door,
Unseen the modest were supplied,
Her constant pity fed the poor,
Then only poor, indeed, the day she died.
And Oh, for this! while sculpture decks thy shrine,
And art exhausts profusion round,   130
The tribute of a tear be mine,
A simple song, a sigh profound.
Their faith shall come, a pilgrim grey,
To bless the tomb that wraps thy clay;
And calm religion shall repair
To dwell a weeping hermit there.
Truth, fortitude, and friendship shall agree
To blend their virtues while they think of thee.

AIR. CHORUS. *Pomposo*

Let us, let all the world agree,
To profit by resembling thee.   140

END OF THE FIRST PART

Part II

OVERTURE PASTORALE
MAN SPEAKER

Fast by that shore where Thames' translucent steam
Reflects new glories on his breast,
Where, splendid as the youthful poet's dream,
He forms a scene beyond Elysium blest;
Where sculptur'd elegance and native grace
Unite to stamp the beauties of the place;
While, sweetly blending, still are seen
The wavy lawn, the sloping green;

While novelty, with cautious cunning,
Through every maze of fancy running,   150
From China borrows aid to deck the scene.
There sorrowing by the river's glassy bed,
Forlorn, a rural band complain'd,
All whom Augusta's bounty fed,
All whom her clemency sustain'd.
The good old sire, unconscious of decay,
The modest matron, clad in home-spun grey,
The military boy, the orphan'd maid,
The shatter'd veteran, now first dismay'd;
These sadly join beside the murmuring deep,   160
And as they view the towers of Kew,
Call on their mistress, now no more, and weep.

CHORUS. *Affettuoso. Largo*

Ye shady walks, ye waving greens,
Ye nodding tow'rs, ye fairy scenes,
Let all your ecchoes now deplore,
That She who form'd your beauties is no more.

MAN SPEAKER

First of the train the patient rustic came,
Whose callous hand had form'd the scene,
Bending at once with sorrow and with age,
With many a tear, and many a sigh between,   170
And where, he cried, shall now my babes have bread,
Or how shall age support its feeble fire?
No lord will take me now, my vigour fled,
Nor can my strength perform what they require:
Each grudging master keeps the labourer bare,
A sleek and idle race is all their care.
My noble mistress thought not so!
Her bounty, like the morning dew,
Unseen, tho' constant, used to flow;
And as my stength decay'd, her bounty grew.   180
In decent dress, and coarsely clean,
The pious matron next was seen,
Clasp'd in her hand a godly book was borne,

By use and daily meditation worn:
That decent dress, this holy guide,
Augusta's care had well supply'd.
And ah! she cries, all woe begone,
What now remains for me?
Oh! where shall weeping want repair
To ask for charity?   190
Too late in life for me to ask,
And shame prevents the deed,
And tardy, tardy are the times
To succour should I need.

   But all my wants, before I spoke,
Were to my mistress known;
She still reliev'd, nor sought my praise,
Contented with her own.
But every day her name I'll bless,
My morning prayer, my evening song,   200
I'll praise her while my life shall last,
A life that cannot last me long.

SONG, BY A WOMAN

Each day, each hour, her name I'll bless,
My morning and my evening song,
And when in death my vows shall cease,
My children shall the note prolong.

MAN SPEAKER

The hardy veteran after struck the sight,
Scarr'd, mangl'd, maim'd in every part,
Lopp'd of his limbs in many a gallant fight,
In nought entire – except his heart: 210
Mute for a while, and sullenly distress'd,
At last the impetuous sorrow fir'd his breast.
Wild is the whirlwind rolling
O'er Afric's sandy plain,
And wild the tempest howling
Along the billow'd main:
But every danger felt before,

The raging deep, the whirlwind's roar,
Less dreadful struck me with dismay,
Than what I feel that fatal day.   220
Oh, let me fly a land that spurns the brave,
Oswego's dreary shores shall be my grave;
I'll seek that less inhospitable coast,
And lay my body where my limbs were lost.

SONG BY A MAN. *Bass. Spirituoso*

Old Edward's sons, unknown to yield,
Shall crowd from Cressy's laurell'd field
To do thy memory right:
For thine and Britain's wrongs they feel,
Again they snatch the gleamy steel,
And wish th' avenging fight.   230

WOMAN SPEAKER

In innocence and youth complaining,
Next appear'd a lovely maid,
Affliction o'er each feature reigning,
Kindly came in beauty's aid;
Every grace that grief dispenses,
Every glance that warms the soul,
In sweet succession charm'd the senses,
While pity harmoniz'd the whole.
The garland of beauty, 'tis thus she would say,
No more shall my crook or my temples adorn,   240
I'll not wear a garland, Augusta's away,
I'll not wear a garland until she return:
But alas! that return I never shall see,
The ecchoes of Thames' shall my sorrows proclaim,
There promis'd a lover to come, but oh me!
'Twas death, 'twas the death of my mistress that came.
But ever, for ever, her image shall last,
I'll strip all the Spring of its earliest bloom;
On her grave shall the cowslip and primrose be cast,
And the new-blossom'd thorn shall whiten her tomb.   250

SONG BY A WOMAN. *Pastorale*

With garlands of beauty the queen of the May
No more will her crook or her temples adorn;
For who'd wear a garland when she is away,
When she is remov'd, and shall never return?

On the grave of Augusta these garlands be plac't,
We'll rifle the Spring of its earliest bloom,
And there shall the cowslip and primrose be cast,
And the new-blossom'd thorn shall whiten her tomb.

CHORUS. *Altro Modo*

On the grave of Augusta this garland be plac't,
We'll rifle the Spring of its earliest bloom
And there shall the cowslip and primrose be cast,
And the tears of her country shall water her tomb.

260

THE END

Song for *She Stoops to Conquer*

Ah me, when shall I marry me?
Lovers are plenty but fail to relieve me;
He, fond youth, that could carry me,
Offers to love but means to deceive me.

But I will rally and combat the ruiner;
Not a look, not a smile shall my passion discover;
She that gives all to the false one pursuing her
Makes but a penitent, loses a lover.

Retaliation

A Poem

Of old, when Scarron his companions invited,
Each guest brought his dish, and the feast was united;
If our landlord supplies us with beef, and with fish,
Let each guest bring himself, and he brings the best dish:
Our Dean shall be venison, just fresh from the plains;
Our Burke shall be tongue, with a garnish of brains;
Our Will shall be wild fowl, of excellent flavour,
And Dick with his pepper, shall heighten their savour:
Our Cumberland's sweet-bread its place shall obtain,
And Douglass's pudding, substantial and plain: 10
Our Garrick's a sallad, for in him we see
Oil, vinegar, sugar, and saltness agree:
To make out the dinner, full certain I am,
That Ridge is anchovy, and Reynolds is lamb;
That Hickey's a capon, and by the same rule,
Magnanimous Goldsmith, a gooseberry fool:
At a dinner so various, at such a repast,
Who'd not be a glutton, and stick to the last:
Here, waiter, more wine, let me sit while I'm able,
'Till all my companions sink under the table;   20
Then with chaos and blunders encircling my head,
Let me ponder, and tell what I think of the dead.

Here lies the good Dean, re-united to earth,
Who mixt reason with pleasure, and wisdom with mirth:
If he had any faults, he has left us in doubt,
At least, in six weeks, I could not find 'em out;
Yet some have declar'd, and it can't be denied 'em,
That sly-boots was cursedly cunning to hide 'em.

Here lies our good Edmund, whose genius was such,
We scarcely can praise it, or blame it too much;   30
Who, born for the Universe, narrow'd his mind,
And to party gave up, what was meant for mankind.
Tho' fraught with all learning, kept straining his throat,

To persuade Tommy Townshend to lend him a vote;
Who, too deep for his hearers, still went on refining,
And thought of convincing, while they thought of dining;

Tho' equal to all things, for all things unfit,
Too nice for a statesman, too proud for a wit:
For a patriot too cool; for a drudge, disobedient,
And too fond of the *right* to pursue the *expedient*.   40
In short, 'twas his fate, unemploy'd, or in place, Sir,
To eat mutton cold, and cut blocks with a razor.

Here lies honest William, whose heart was a mint,
While the owner ne'er knew half the good that was in't;
The pupil of impulse, it forc'd him along,
His conduct still right, with his argument wrong;
Still aiming at honour, yet fearing to roam,
The coachman was tipsy, the chariot drove home;
Would you ask for his merits, alas! he had none,
What was good was spontaneous, his faults were his own.   50

Here lies honest Richard, whose fate I must sigh at,
Alas, that such frolic should now be so quiet!
What spirits were his, what wit and what whim,
Now breaking a jest, and now breaking a limb;
Now rangling and grumbling to keep up the ball,
Now teazing and vexing, yet laughing at all?
In short so provoking a Devil was Dick,
That we wish'd him full ten times a day at Old Nick,
But missing his mirth and agreeable vein,
As often we wish'd to have Dick back again.   60

Here Cumberland lies having acted his parts,
The Terence of England, the mender of hearts;
A flattering painter, who made it his care
To draw men as they ought to be, not as they are.
His gallants are all faultless, his women divine,
And comedy wonders at being so fine;
Like a tragedy queen he has dizen'd her out,
Or rather like tragedy giving a rout.
His fools have their follies so lost in a croud

Of virtues and feelings, that folly grows proud,   70
And coxcombs alike in their failings alone,
Adopting his portraits are pleas'd with their own.
Say, where has our poet this malady caught,
Or wherefore his characters thus without fault?
Say was it that vainly directing his view,
To find out mens' virtues and finding them few,
Quite sick of pursuing each troublesome elf,
He grew lazy at last and drew from himself?

   Here Douglas retires from his toils to relax,
The scourge of impostors, the terror of quacks: 80
Come all ye quack bards, and ye quacking divines,
Come and dance on the spot where your tyrant reclines,
When Satire and Censure encircl'd his throne,
I fear'd for your safety, I fear'd for my own;
But now he is gone, and we want a detector,
Our Dodds shall be pious, our Kenricks shall lecture;
Macpherson write bombast, and call it a style,
Our Townshend make speeches, and I shall compile;
New Lauders and Bowers the Tweed shall cross over,
No countryman living their tricks to discover;   90
Detection her taper shall quench to a spark,
And Scotchman meet Scotchman and cheat in the dark.

   Here lies David Garrick, describe me who can,
An abridgment of all that was pleasant in man;
As an actor, confest without rival to shine,
As a wit, if not first, in the very first line,
Yet with talents like these, and an excellent heart,
The man had his failings, a dupe to his art;
Like an ill judging beauty, his colours he spread,
And beplaister'd, with rouge, his own natural red.   100
On the stage he was natural, simple, affecting,
'Twas only that, when he was off, he was acting:
With no reason on earth to go out of his way,
He turn'd and he varied full ten times a day;
Tho' secure of our hearts, yet confoundedly sick,
If they were not his own by finessing and trick,

He cast off his friends, as a huntsman his pack;
For he knew when he pleased he could whistle them back.
Of praise, a mere glutton, he swallowed what came,
And the puff of a dunce, he mistook it for fame; 110
'Till his relish grown callous, almost to disease,
Who pepper'd the highest, was surest to please.
But let us be candid, and speak out our mind,
If dunces applauded, he paid them in kind.
Yet Kenricks, ye Kellys, and Woodfalls so grave,
What a commerce was yours, while you got and you gave?
How did Grub-street re-echo the shouts that you rais'd,
While he was beroscius'd, and you were beprais'd?
But peace to his spirit, wherever it flies,
To act as an angel, and mix with the skies: 120
Those poets, who owe their best fame to his skill,
Shall still be his flatterers, go where he will.
Old Shakespeare receive him with praise and with love,
And Beaumonts and Bens be his Kellys above.

    Here Hickey reclines, a most blunt, pleasant creature,
And slander itself must allow him good-nature:
He cherish'd his friend, and he relish'd a bumper;
Yet one fault he had, and that one was a thumper:
Perhaps you may ask if that man was a miser?
I answer, no, no, for he always was wiser; 130
Too courteous, perhaps, or obligingly flat;
His very worst foe can't accuse him of that.
Perhaps he confided in men as they go,
And so was too foolishly honest; ah, no.
Then what was his failing? come tell it, and burn ye,
He was, could he help it? a special attorney.

    Here Reynolds is laid, and to tell you my mind,
He has not left a better or wiser behind;
His pencil was striking, resistless and grand,
His manners were gentle, complying and bland; 140
Still born to improve us in every part,
His pencil our faces, his manners our heart:
To coxcombs averse, yet most civilly staring,
When they judged without skill he was still hard of hearing:

When they talk'd of their Raphaels, Corregios and stuff,
He shifted his trumpet, and only took snuff.

THE END

Notes

Several collected editions of Goldsmith's poems and other works were published soon after his death in 1774. His *Works* were printed both in London and in Dublin in 1775, 1777 and again in 1780. Thomas Percy's *Life of Dr Oliver Goldsmith* first appeared in the four-volume *Miscellaneous Works* printed in 1801. The notes to the present edition are indebted to Roger Lonsdale's superb and authoritative *Poems of Thomas Gray, William Collins and Oliver Goldsmith* (1969) and to Tom Davis's 1975 Everyman edition of Goldsmith's *Poems and Plays*.

On a Beautiful Youth Struck Blind With Lightning: First printed 6 October 1759, and noted to have been 'Imitated from the SPANISH'. The original source has not been identified. **l. 4 Narcissus' fate:** the beautiful Boeotian youth Narcissus, having glimpsed his own reflection in a fountain's pool, fell in love with the inaccessible image and eventually, in despair, killed himself.

The Gift: First printed 13 October 1759. A loose imitation of Bernard de la Monnoye's 1715 'Etrène à Iris'. **l. 1 cruel Iris:** the Bow Street, Covent Garden (London) address of the poem's subject as well as her designation as a 'mercenary beauty' suggests that Iris is either an actress, or a prostitute, or both.

A Sonnet: First printed 20 October 1759. An imitation of the seventeenth-century French poet Denis Sanguin de Saint-Pavin's 'Iris tremble qu'au premier jour'. The poem is, strictly speaking, a sonnet only in the sense of being a 'little song'.

An Elegy on that Glory of her Sex Mrs Mary Blaize: First printed 27 October 1759. The periodic bathos of the poem is based on the model of Bernard de la Monnoye's 1716 'Le Fameux La Galisse'. **l. 26 Kent-Street:** Southwark street notorious for its tramps and beggars.

The Double Transformation: A Tale: First printed 6 January 1760.

Although not based on any one particular model, the work recalls several of
Jonathan Swift's satirical poems in octasyllabic couplets, such as 'Phyllis, or
the Progress of Love' (1719). **l. 8 a knowing one:** i.e. one who was 'in the
know', not so much intellectually as socially or in sporting and practical
matters. **l. 64: patching:** putting small patches on the face by way of
fashionable adornment (this example is cited in the *OED*). **l. 94 phyz:** i.e.
'phiz', popular slang for 'physiognomy' or facial expression. **l. 97 nooze:**
i.e., noose. To be 'noosed' was to be married.

Description of an Author's Bed-Chamber: First printed 2 May 1760.
Goldsmith had sent his brother Henry a fragment corresponding to ll. 7–18
of the poem as it was finally published as early as January 1759, as a
specimen of an 'heroicomical' poem he claimed then to be writing. **l. 3
Calvert's butt, and Parson's black champaign:** Calvert and Parsons
were London brewers. 'Butt' and 'black champagne' were popular
designations for the type of rich porter they brewed. **l. 4 Drury lane:** the
popular haunt of prostitutes. **l. 11 The royal game of goose:** a popular
board game. **l. 12 the twelve rules the royal martyr drew:** the twelve
rules or admonitory precepts supposedly drawn up by the 'royal martyr'
Charles I and discovered among his possessions after his death. **l. 14 brave
Prince William shew'd his lamp-black face:** a silhouette of William
Augustus, Duke of Cumberland, who became a popular hero after he
defeated the Scots at Culloden Moor in April 1746. Like the print depicting
the twelve rules of Charles I mentioned above (note to l. 12), such a
representation would have been recognized by contemporary readers of the
poem as common but rather old fashioned and out of date.

On Seeing Mrs *, Perform in the Character of ****:*** First printed 21
October 1760. The poem was intended to be a parody of the 'flaunting' but
predictable praise included in newspaper verses which generally followed
the first appearance of a new actress on the London stage. **l. 1 the nine:** i.e.
the nine Muses. **l. 9 Paphian groves:** Paphos, on the island of Cyprus, was
sacred to the 'queen of love', Venus.

On the Death of the Right Honourable ***: First printed 4 March 1761.
Like the *Elegy on Mary Blaize* (see p. 4 and note p. 81), a parody and attack
on 'premeditated flattery' in the manner of La Monnoye's 'Le Fameux La
Galisse'.

An Elegy on the Death of a Mad Dog: First printed 27 March 1766, when it was included in *The Vicar of Wakefield*. The poem is the third of Goldsmith's parodies in the mock-panegyric or mock-elegiac mode. **l. 5 Isling town:** Islington, in the mid-eighteenth century, although still considered to be (in Goldsmith's own words) a 'pretty neat town', was often the butt of satire directed at the insipidity of 'country' life close to the metropolis. **l. 15 mungrel:** i.e., mongrel.

***Song from* The Vicar of Wakefield:** First printed 27 March 1766, in Chapter 24 of Goldsmith's novel, *The Vicar of Wakefield*, where it is sung by Dr Primrose's second child and eldest daughter, Olivia.

***Edwin and Angelina: A Ballad*:** First printed in a private, undated edition dedicated to the Countess of Northumberland and subsequently, in 1766, included (with revisions and alterations) in Chapter 8 of *The Vicar of Wakefield* (1766) in the course of Mr Burchill's attack on modern English poetry. The ballad is in fact presented in the novel as a corrective example of solid English verse to be contrasted to the plotless, fragmented and overly-luxuriant products of most contemporary English writers. **ll. 31–2 'Man wants but little here below,/Nor wants that little long':** see Edward Young's *Night Thoughts* (1742–5), Book IV, l. 119: 'Man wants but little, nor that little, long.' **l. 101 the Tyne:** the Tyne river, in the north of England.

***The Captivity: An Oratorio*:** Written some time before 31 October 1764, when Goldsmith sold the libretto to James Dodsley and John Newbery for ten guineas. The oratorio was not printed in Goldsmith's lifetime (it was finally included in an 1820 edition of his *Miscellaneous Works*). The captivity referred to in the work's title is the deportation of the Jews following the destruction of Jerusalem in 588 BC. The action of the oratorio takes place *c*. 539–38 BC, when Cyrus, the King of Persia, conquered Babylon and ended the captivity, and a group of exiles led by one Sheshbazzar prepared to return to Jerusalem. **l. 182 Zedekiah's fall:** the deposition, in 587 BC, of king Zedekiah of Judah, who had been enthroned by Babylon.

***The Traveller, or A Prospect of Society*:** First printed 19 December 1764. The poem was begun almost ten years earlier, while Goldsmith was travelling on the Continent in 1755, and an early draft of some portion of the poem ('about two hundred lines', according to one source) was sent to his brother Henry while he was still abroad. Goldsmith revised the work substantially between 1762 and 1764, and appears to have been paid twenty guineas for the finished product. Acknowledging that the piece could well prove instrumental in establishing his reputation as anything other than a literary 'hack', Goldsmith took great pains in revising the work. He solicited the help of his friend Samuel Johnson who, after Goldsmith's death, cautiously admitted having contributed (at least) ll. 420, 429–34 and 437–8. **Dedication: Rev. Henry Goldsmith:** Goldsmith's eldest brother (d. 1768), curate of Kilkenny West, near Lissoy, in County Westmeath, Ireland. **Poem: l. 2 lazy Scheld, or wandering Po:** the Scheldt is a river in northern France which enters the sea at Antwerp. The Po is a river in northern Italy – the country's largest – which empties into the Adriatic near Ferrara. **l. 3: Carinthian boor:** Carinthia was a Hapsburg Duchy in the South Austrian Alps. Goldsmith's rather unfair and atypical characterization of the inhabitants of Carinthia as 'boors' appears to have been the result of his own anecdotal experiences while travelling through and seeking accommodation in the region. **l. 5 Campania's plain:** the 'Campagna' of western Italy, famous in Roman times for its extraordinary richness and fertility. At the time of Goldsmith's own travels in the mid-eighteenth century, the area was comparatively unpeopled and desolate. **l. 69 the line:** i.e. the Equator. **l. 84 Idra's cliffs as Arno's shelvy side:** Goldsmith's 'Idra' remains elusive. He may have been referring to Lake Idro, near Brescia, in northern Italy, or – more likely – to the mining town of Idria, in the Austrian Alps (hence the location's 'cliffs'). The Arno is the temperamental river which flows through Florence and enters the Gulf of Genoa near Pisa. **l. 105 Appennine:** The Apennines, which stretch southward from the Alps forming the historically and demographically consequential 'backbone' of Italy. **l. 170 man and steel . . . sword:** i.e. mercenary soldiers. **l. 244 murmuring Loire:** the Loire river, flowing through central France. **l. 320 Hydaspis:** the Hydaspes – now called the Jhilum – a river in India mentioned by Horace in his *Odes* (I. xxii). **ll. 411–12 wild Oswego . . . Niagara:** the Oswego is a river in Canada which runs into Lake Ontario. The great falls at Niagara were close by a fort and settlement which had been surrendered by the French to British forces in 1759. **l. 436 Luke's iron crown . . . steel:** György Dosa was the leader of an Hungarian uprising against the Turks in 1513. He was eventually captured and cruelly punished by being made to wear a red-hot iron crown and sit on a red-hot throne. Goldsmith here substitutes the name of Dosa's brother – Luke – for that of György (which is anglicized as 'George') perhaps to avoid any possible application of the reference to King George III. Robert-François Damiens, who in 1757 attempted to assassinate

King Louis XV of France, was chained to a 'bed of steel' and tortured mercilessly before finally being executed.

A New Simile. In the Manner of Swift: First printed 3 June 1765. The poem is not, in fact, an imitation of Swift's work at all, but rather of Thomas Sheridan's *A New Simile for the Ladies* (1732). Sheridan's work had prompted a reply from Swift – *An Answer to a Scandalous Poem* (1732) – and the two were subsequently printed together in editions of Swift's own poetical *Works*. **l. 6 A chapter ... Pantheon:** Andrew Tooke's *The Pantheon, Representing the Fabulous Histories of the Heathen Gods and Most Illustrious Heroes* (1698) was a popular school text, illustrated with numerous copper-plate engravings, including that of 'Mercurius' or Mercury used here by Goldsmith (l. 10). **l. 33: caducis:** i.e. caduceus, Mercury's 'wand' or rod, the touch of which could induce sleep in mortals. **l. 52 drove souls to Tart'rus:** referring to Mercury's capacity as 'psycho-pomp', or one who leads souls through the underworld. **l. 64 senseless stones and blocks:** Mercury exists in this world only as a stone statue, a possible reference to the *hermae* of classical antiquity as described by Tooke in his *Pantheon*.

Verses in Reply to an Invitation to Dinner at Dr Baker's: Written on 20 January 1767, and first printed in 1837 in a collected edition of Goldsmith's *Works*. Dr George Baker was physician to Sir Joshua Reynolds. **ll. 11–18 Horneck and Nesbitt ... Kauffmann ... the Jessamy bride ... the Reynoldses two ... Little Comedy ... the Captain:** all members of Sir Joshua's social 'circle': Mrs Hannah Horneck and her daughter Mary (the 'Jessamy' or fashionable bride); Mrs Susannah Nesbitt (sister of the brewer Henry Thrale); the famous painter Angelica Kauffman; Sir Joshua and his sister Frances; Catherine Horneck ('Little Comedy') and her brother Charles ('the Captain'). **l. 36 Your Devonshire crew:** Reynolds had been born (1723) at Plympton, in Devon. **l. 44 today's *Advertiser*:** a poem complimentary to both Reynolds and Kauffmann had appeared in that day's issue of the *Public Advertiser* (20 January 1767).

Epitaph on Edward Purdon: Written soon after Purdon's death on 27 March 1767, and first printed with Goldsmith's other works in Edmond Malone's edition of the collected *Poems and Plays* (1777). Purdon had been a fellow of Goldsmith's at Trinity College, Dublin. At the time of his sudden death, he had been living in Smithfield and making ends meet with his productions as a writer, editor and translator.

***Epilogue to* The Sister: A Comedy:** Written for Charlotte Lennox's *The Sister*, which was performed only once, on 18 February 1768, at Covent Garden, London. The epilogue was printed several times in unauthorized newspaper editions before *The Sister* was published in its entirety on 3 March 1769. Lennox's play, which was a dramatized version of her 1758 novel *Henrietta*, was hissed from the stage by a cabal of self-appointed critics who did not agree with the author's criticisms of Shakespeare in her *Shakespear Illustrated* (1753–4). **l. 17 Hebes:** Hebe, daughter of Juno and cup-bearer to the gods, was sometimes called the goddess of youth. Goldsmith uses the name here ironically.

***The Deserted Village*:** First published 26 May 1770, and written between 1768 and 1770, although Goldsmith had been turning over the general concerns of the poem in his mind for close to a decade. The poem was an immediate popular success and attracted attention both for its considera-tion of the theme of rural depopulation and for its extraordinary and lovingly nostalgic evocation of English country life. **Dedication: Sir Joshua Reynolds:** the distinguished artist Joshua Reynolds (1723–92) had been Goldsmith's close friend since their first meeting in 1761. **l. 9 my brother:** i.e. Henry Goldsmith, to whom the poet had dedicated *The Traveller* (see p. 30 and note p. 83). Henry Goldsmith died in 1768. **Poem: l. 1 Auburn:** Although the description of Goldsmith's village may in some respects have been inspired by his own childhood memories of Lissoy, in County Westmeath, Ireland, no specific location is meant here. England boasts two genuine 'Auburns' – one in Wiltshire and another in Lincolnshire. **ll. 227–36 The white-washed wall . . . glistened in a row:** Goldsmith draws on his own *Description of an Author's Bed-Chamber* (see p. 9 and note p. 82). **l. 344 wild Altama:** the Altamah river in the state of Georgia, North America. **l. 418 Torno's cliffs, or Pambamarca's side:** Torne (or Tornea) denotes a lake, river and town in Sweden. Pambamarca is a mountain in what is today Ecuador. **l. 419 equinoctial fervours:** i.e. the heats typical of lands situated at or near the Equator. **ll. 427–30 That trade's . . . and the sky:** Samuel Johnson marked these closing four lines in Boswell's copy of the work as having been his own contribution to Goldsmith's poem.

***Epitaph on Thomas Parnell*:** First published in 1776, though probably written originally in connection with an edition of Parnell's *Poems* on which Goldsmith was working in 1770. Parnell (1679–1718) was a Dublin native and a member of the Scriblerus Club. Most of his work was published posthumously by Alexander Pope in 1721. Despite the opening line of Goldsmith's poem, the verses were not inscribed on Parnell's tomb.

The Haunch of Venison. A Poetical Epistle to Lord Clare: First printed in 1776. Written some time between October 1770, and January 1771. The poem is addressed to the Vice-Treasurer for Ireland, Robert Nugent, Viscount Clare, who had cultivated Goldsmith's acquaintance following the publication of *The Traveller* in 1764. In addition to his several government appointments and positions, Clare was an amateur poet who had contributed to Dodsley's popular 1748 *Collection of Poems* (2nd edn). The poem may have been prompted by an actual gift of venison, although aspects of the work find their source in satires by Boileau and, ultimately, Horace. **l. 14 bounce:** lie, imposition. **l. 18 Mr Burn:** Clare's nephew, Michael Byrne, an Irishman familiar with the custom of the country. **l. 21 Reynolds:** Sir Joshua Reynolds (see note to the Dedication, *The Deserted Village*, p. 86). **l. 24 Monroe's:** Dorothy Monroe, a celebrated beauty. **l. 27 Howard and Coley and Haworth and Hiff:** hack writers. **l. 29 my country man Higgins:** probably the 'Captain Higgins' who was a friend of Goldsmith's, known only for being in the poet's company when he engaged in a fight with the publisher Thomas Evans in 1773. **l. 49 Johnson and Burke:** Samuel Johnson (1709–84) and Edmund Burke (1729–97). **l. 55 mile end:** at the time a small hamlet to the east of London. **l. 60 And nobody with me at Sea but myself:** an absurd phrase which became popular in the period and which originated in the trial of Henry Frederick, Duke of Cumberland, for adultery with Lady Grosvenor. One of the Duke's letters produced as evidence in the course of the trial contained a passage in which the Duke described awakening from a dream to find 'nobody by me by myself at Sea'. The Duke's poor writing and apparent illiteracy was the source of much popular, humorous comment. **l. 72 the other with Thrale:** Samuel Johnson was at this period spending much of his time with his new acquaintance, Henry Thrale, at the latter's home at Streatham. **ll. 77–8 the snarler . . . the scourge . . . Cinna . . . Panurge:** newspaper pen-names. **l. 95: chocolate:** dark or chocolate coloured. **ll. 109–10 A visage so sad . . . curtains by night:** a reference to Shakespeare's *II Henry IV*, I.i.70–3: 'Even such a man, so faint, so spiritless,/So dull, so dead in look, so woe-begone,/Drew Priam's curtains in the dead of night,/And would have told him half his Troy was burnt'. The lines are addressed by the Earl of Northumberland to Morton.

Prologue to **Zobeide:** First printed 19 December 1771. The prologue was written for the premiere performance of Joseph Cradock's tragedy *Zobeide* (an adaptation of Voltaire's *Les Scythes*) at London's Covent Garden on 11 December that same year. **ll. 1–8 In these bold times . . . hoity-toity queens:** a reference to the voyages of Captain Cook, whose expeditions to the South Seas were the source of tremendous popular interest. Cook's *Endeavour* had sailed to Tahiti in 1768 to mark the transit of **Venus** (l. 4), and had returned to England in July 1771. Samuel Johnson had memorably devalued the contributions of the botanists Joseph Banks and Daniel Solander to Cook's explorations of discovery by suggesting that they had fulfilled their role in the voyage merely by culling 'simples' (l. 6) or curative herbs. **l. 11 *Scythian stores*:** a reference to the setting of Cradock's tragedy, in Scythia. **l. 28 palaver:** rudimentary speech or communication. **l. 32 His honour is no mercenary trader:** Cradock, himself wealthy, donated the profits of his tragedy to the leading lady, Mrs Yates.

***Threnodia Augustalis*:** First printed and performed on 20 February 1772. The work – which Goldsmith himself dismissed as the product of 'little more than two days' effort – was not collected with the poet's other writings until 1810. The piece was written to be performed at a concert at Carlisle House in Soho Square, London in memory of Augusta, the widow of Frederick, Prince of Wales, and mother to King George III. The Princess Dowager had died on 8 February 1772. Goldsmith's title recalls John Dryden's 1685 *Threnodia Augustalis*, the 'Funeral-Pindarique' which had rather more carefully and sincerely commemorated the death of Charles II. **ll. 141–51 Fast by that shore . . . deck the scene:** a description of Kew Gardens, recently redesigned and fashioned in the popular 'oriental' manner. **ll. 225–6 Old Edward's sons . . . Cressy's laurell'd field:** Edward III (1327–77) who memorably defeated the French cavalry under Philip VI at the battle of Crécy in 1346.

***Song for* She Stoops to Conquer:** First printed two months after Goldsmith's death, in June 1774, and written some time before March 1773, when *She Stoops to Conquer* premiered at London's Covent Garden. The song, preserved by James Boswell, was written for the character of Miss Hardcastle but, as Boswell observed, 'it was left out, as Mrs Bulkeley who played the part did not sing'.

***Retaliation*:** First printed on 19 April 1774 from a manuscript copy left unfinished at Goldsmith's death. Early in 1774, while Goldsmith was in fact suffering from the illness which would soon lead to his death, a group of his friends – not realizing the serious nature of his condition – took advantage of his absence from one of their informal meetings to amuse themselves by composing mock epitaphs for the poet. David Garrick's contribution – 'Here lies Nolly Goldsmith, for shortness called Noll,/Who wrote like an angel but talked like poor Poll' – achieved some currency after Goldsmith's death. *Retaliation* is Goldsmith's attempt to answer each of the 'wits' in kind. **l. 1 Scarron:** the seventeenth-century French poet and satirist Paul Scarron (1610–60). **l. 3 our landlord:** i.e. of the Saint James's coffee-house, where the club of wits held their occasional meetings. **l. 5 Our Dean:** Doctor Barnard, Dean of Derry. **l. 6 Our Burke:** Edmund Burke **l. 7 Our Will:** William Burke, M.P. A distant relation of Edmund Burke's. **l. 8 Our Dick:** Richard Burke, brother to Edmund, Collector of Customs in Grenada. **l. 9 Our Cumberland:** Richard Cumberland, dramatist, author of *The West Indian* (1771) and *The Fashionable Lover* (1772). **l. 10 Our Douglass:** Dr John Douglas, Canon of Windsor and later Bishop of Carlisle (1787) and Salisbury (1791). **l. 11 Our Garrick:** David Garrick. **l. 14 Ridge . . . Reynolds:** John Ridge (Edmund Burke's lawyer) and Sir Joshua Reynolds. **l. 15 Hickey:** Joseph Hickey, an attorney and legal adviser to Burke. **l. 34 Tommy Townshend:** Thomas Townshend (1733–1800), M.P. for Whitechurch. **l. 42 cut blocks with a razor:** i.e. use the improper tools for the job, hence, waste one's time or misapply one's talent. **ll. 61–78:** Cumberland was an exponent of sentimental comedy, of which the roman dramatist **Terence** (l. 62) was invoked by some as a predecessor. **l. 86 Dodds . . . Kenricks:** William Dodds (1729–77), preacher and author, and William Kenrick (1725?–79), miscellaneous writer, were both types of frauds or hypocrites. **l. 87 Macpherson:** James Macpherson (1736–96), 'translator' of the controversial 'Ossian' poems and – in 1773 – of a prose translation of Homer's *Iliad*. **l. 88 Townshend make speeches, and I shall compile:** Townshend in 1774 made a speech in the House of Commons criticizing the donation of a pension to be awarded to Samuel Johnson. To 'compile' was to gather together other writers' material, i.e. to plagiarize. **l. 89 Lauders and Bowers:** William Lauders (d. 1771) and Archibald Bowers (1686–1766), both fraudulent Scots. Lauders had accused John Milton of plagiarizing *Paradise Lost*. Bowers was a Roman Catholic who attempted to pass himself off in his writings as a member of the Church of England. **l. 115 Kenricks . . . Kellys . . . Woodfalls:** all flatterers and hangers-on of Garricks. On Kenrick see l. 86 and note above. Hugh Kelly's 1768 *False Delicacy* (produced by Garrick) was a huge success as a sentimental comedy. William Woodfall (1746–1803) was a drama critic whose work appeared in, among other publications, the *Public*

Advertiser and the *Morning Chronicle*. **l. 118 beroscius'd:** Charles Church-
ill's *Rosciad* (1761) was a satire on acting, taking its name from one of the
most famous comic actors of antiquity, Roscius. **l. 124 Beaumonts and
Bens:** Francis Beaumont (1584–1616) and Ben Jonson (1572/3–1637),
both famous dramatists of the early seventeenth century. **ll. 145–6 When
they talk'd . . . only took snuff:** Reynolds, who was hard of hearing, used
an ear trumpet and was known to take a great quantity of snuff. Raphael
and Antonio Correggio were famous painters of the Italian Renaissance.

Everyman's Poetry

Titles available in this series

William Blake
ed. Peter Butter
0 460 87800 X

The Brontës
ed. Pamela Norris
0 460 87864 6

Rupert Brooke & Wilfred Owen
ed. George Walter
0 460 87801 8

Robert Burns
ed. Donald Low
0 460 87814 X

Lord Byron
ed. Jane Stabler
0 460 87810 7

John Clare
ed. R. K. R. Thornton
0 460 87823 9

Samuel Taylor Coleridge
ed. John Beer
0 460 87826 3

Four Metaphysical Poets
ed. Douglas Brooks-Davies
0 460 87857 3

Oliver Goldsmith
ed. Robert L. Mack
0 460 87827 1

Thomas Gray
ed. Robert Mack
0 460 87805 0

Ivor Gurney
ed. George Walter
0 460 87797 6

Heinrich Heine
ed. T. J. Reed & David Cram
0 460 87865 4

George Herbert
ed. D. J. Enright
0 460 87795 X

Robert Herrick
ed. Douglas Brooks-Davies
0 460 87799 2

John Keats
ed. Nicholas Roe
0 460 87808 5

Henry Wadsworth Longfellow
ed. Anthony Thwaite
0 460 87821 2

Andrew Marvell
ed. Gordon Campbell
0 460 87812 3

John Milton
ed. Gordon Campbell
0 460 87813 1

Edgar Allan Poe
ed. Richard Gray
0 460 87804 2

Poetry Please!
Foreword by Charles Causley
0 460 87824 7

Alexander Pope
ed. Douglas Brooks-Davies
0 460 87798 4

Alexander Pushkin
ed. A. D. P. Briggs
0 460 87862 X

Lord Rochester
ed. Paddy Lyons
0 460 87819 0

Christina Rossetti
ed. Jan Marsh
0 460 87820 4

William Shakespeare
ed. Martin Dodsworth
0 460 87815 8

John Skelton
ed. Greg Walker
0 460 87796 8

Alfred, Lord Tennyson
ed. Michael Baron
0 460 87802 6

R. S. Thomas
ed. Anthony Thwaite
0 460 87811 5

Walt Whitman
ed. Ellman Crasnow
0 460 87825 5

Oscar Wilde
ed. Robert Mighall
0 460 87803 4